Go 4 It:
A Guide on How to Boost Your Self Esteem, Face
Challenges, Set Up Goals and Accomplish Them

By Jamie CL Miller

Distributed by: Amazon
ISBN: 9781980971320

Copyright and disclosure

TABLE OF CONTENTS

WELCOME   3

WHERE IT STARTS FROM   11

KILLING THE MONSTER   51

GO FOR IT!   79

QA: RISKS AND SAFETY NETS   93

FINAL WORD   105

Welcome

Life might not be as you imagined it

As children, most of us wanted to grow up to become astronauts, ballerinas, and superheroes. Imagination ran wild, and everything was possible. Conquering the highest mountain was no different from an everyday challenge and, courage and energy were the most important qualities to value. But everybody loses the innocence of believing that fairy tales might become real. Aging was a process that took place while you didn't even pay attention. It just happened and, one day, like overnight, you realized strange and new ideas appeared in your mind. You, as all people do, began wanting relationships, started to crave for lust and fortune, discovered pain in many ways and realized what being responsible or being held accountable actually means.

Life is on fast forward. This is how everybody does it nowadays. You start the day early, grab a bite, go to work, follow your schedules and your chores, smile to be polite, say "yes" to please and to cope. You have an endless list of responsibilities that need to be checked as "done"... and most days you just want to collapse into your bed to sleep as if there's no tomorrow.

Your bed is not the refuge you run to for safety and relief. You're simply lying to yourself if you think that. You might sleep 6-8 or even 12 hours... but you will still have to get up to the same problems and face the same demons. Being an adult is tiresome and maybe not that pleasant. Sometimes, it's just an endless marathon of getting things done and keeping appearances up. Yet, it happens.

You're more unique than you think, less alone than you know

Your mother might have told you that you're the apple of her eye. Maybe you've been spoilt as a child and lived to think everything can be accomplished with some effort. Later on, school encouraged you to dream big and see yourself reaching a higher standard of performance, while receiving appreciation for whom you are, exactly as you are.

In time, you discovered that you have at least a few qualities you are aware of and can rely on. And so, you were ready. You had great expectations, but yet you were not prepared or experienced enough for what would come later. And who would have imagined what was to come? Life threw its dirt in your face with its random, insensible and unforgivingly harsh ways. You bottled up and hid from the world; nobody actually knows what happened to you and who you would end up to be. Your true self and some of your most burning goals were not accomplished. They might have actually been put on hold or lost on some empty, dusty shelf of forgotten, delusive hopes.

You're not the only one feeling like this. Being put down by life is not uncommon. Feeling that there is no hope or nothing much to do in some situations is perfectly normal as it happens to most people. Hard times, with all the pain and sorrow they bring along, are natural. They come to hurt, to keep you down, but they also bring experience and knowledge that you couldn't gain any other way. And this special type of knowledge is something special, as it's earned and paid for with pieces of your soul, months of your life. Don't despair, take it as it is.

The skepticism and opposition towards change are not uncommon

Changes scare most people. Each change might come with some uncertainty, with some risks and hidden issues that you could not take into account right from the start. So the reluctance to change doesn't make you weak, or a coward. The mind has its defense mechanisms that keep you on a steady track for your own protection.

Change your opinions, keep to your principles; change your leaves, keep intact your roots.
Victor Hugo, 1772-1821 (French poet, novelist, and dramatist)

With this book, you won't be pushed to aim for revolutionary changes that require advanced power and concentration you might not have at your disposal for the moment. The purpose is not to mobilize you towards actions that would abruptly transform you into a new person. This wouldn't do you any good because the final goal is not to bend your will, your needs, or your personality on the way. You will read and explore methods on how to focus more on the willingness and capacity to adapt to different environments, and about the power to be flexible when the external factors require it.

You will read about feelings, difficulties, and explore the pain and the darkness to find the needs and logic everybody harbors deep down. You'll be shown how to set goals, make plans and debate on how to stick to them better.

That's why you need small but solid steps

Continue reading to discover what are actually the most important aspects of your life that you need to focus on to have a clear mindset, and be able to establish and reach goals.

Keep your mind open about an organized day-to-day plan, and be receptive to the power of positive thinking and the given examples. Treat this book with care and let it be your guide towards more serene feelings and a reliable, logical plan to accomplish the goals that determine you as a unique, ambitious, and successful person. Remember that your qualities never fade. You sometimes just forget how to activate them and make the best use of them to enjoy life to its fullest.

There is no such thing as failure. Life sometimes gives you setbacks. It reminds you to be humble, to sit and contemplate, to cope, to support and reinvent yourself based on newly accumulated experiences. It's a continuous learning process people sometimes don't fully understand. But, just wait. Just breathe. Let yourself be carried away. With each day you are better - you know more, you experience more - you have more and more resources in order to adjust, to act, and to win.

If some things simply don't work out, maybe it's because you were not completely ready and you didn't realize what it takes to be ready. Don't give up, go forward. Learn more, try again, and you will surely make it.

This is how this book will help you

Start with the "WHY": Here you will explore the reasons due to which you are currently facing issues determining your goals and/or accomplishing them, understand the root causes, and see if keeping some habits or mental constructs might help you or not.

Continue with the "HOW": Here you will analyze psychological factors and real-life situations in order to see yourself from the outside, and better understand where you stand compared to where you want to go.

And then "JUST DO IT": In the end, you will be guided to take a leap of faith in enrolling for an organized, self-managed and do-it-at-home program that should bring you awareness and clarity in making decisions. You should be able to find the power to cleverly and successfully reach your goals in a short period of time.

As already discussed, you will not be alone in this. **Make the best of this guide and use its resources:**

- **Chapter recaps:** At the end of each chapter you will find a short recap that will help you memorize the most important and useful ideas. But, don't skip to the end of the chapters as the stories, examples, and explanations within will depict situations and mental constructs you wouldn't otherwise fully understand.
- **Actionable plan:** This book is not just some description of why you haven't been yourself in a while. While wanting to understand the WHY, you will be guided to focus on what should be done to change these unpleasant situations. So, you will receive directions and solutions that should fit almost anyone interested in boosting their self-esteem and, in the end, life.
- **FAQ section:** If some ideas or to-does might seem ambiguous, don't stress. The list of the most frequently asked questions is here, with extra explanations to complete your understanding of debatable issues. Once you have finished the book, you should feel better; it will guide and support you

all the way until you are happy with your decisions or general well-being.

Believe it or not, you're halfway there

So, you're not happy with the way some things are going for you at the moment. You decided you want more and you're at least interested, if not fully determined, to try out something new in order to change the status quo.

You're part of those about whom people usually say *"they make it through life."* You're aware of all the good and bad happening to you, or around you, and you simply don't want to settle for *"that's it"* and take it for granted. That's why you started reading this book in the first place: because you can, and you know you can, accomplish more for yourself. Your curiosity for experimenting with new ideas and your eagerness to improve yourself shows that you don't just want more… but that you also deserve more. Because, in all that surrounds us, success is dedicated to those who are solution oriented, who sometimes fail, but keep trying - people like you.

Let's not lose any time, and now start focusing on the common goal: aiming high and actually getting to where you want to be.

Thank you for being here and good luck!

Where it starts from

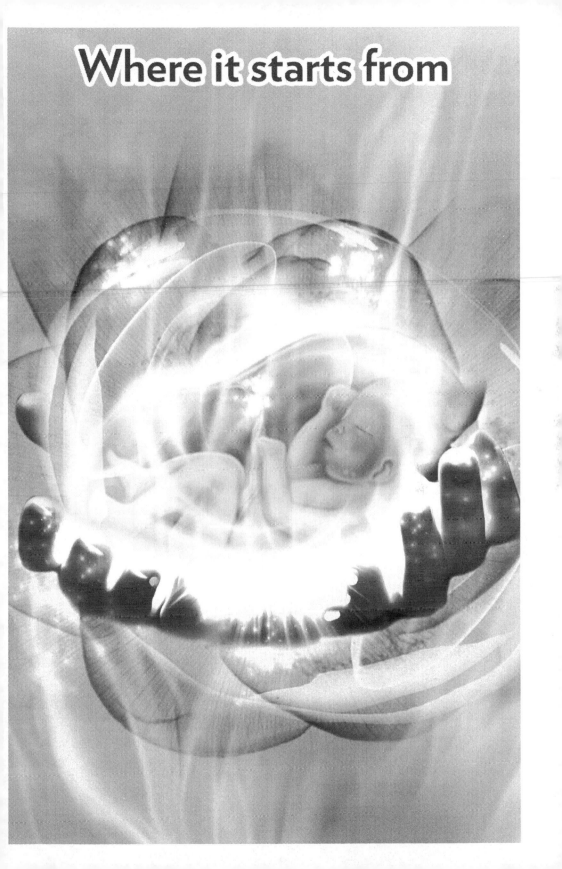

Where it starts from

The Pyramid of Needs

Imagine yourself calm and peaceful, no care in the world. All is good and well. You have no needs, no plans to make, no battles to fight. It's all safe, quiet and peaceful like in an idyllic mother's womb. Could this state of perfect balance be regained?

NO! And get used to it. You are an adult; you will never regain the worry-free state of mind you had as a child. Childhood is over and, if you were lucky to have a fortunate one, those happy days remain as memories and a thing of the past. You will never again find the innocence, and lack of responsibility childhood brought.

As people grow and develop into adults, they develop by learning within the social context they are being brought up in. Everybody starts within their family, and the values they are being taught at home. They continue to learn during school, and within the groups of friends and acquaintances frequented the most. This is how people gain the notion of concepts such as family, love, care, fairness, religion, and others. Comparing yourself with those around you, and the most appreciated values of the groups you belong to and societies you live in will also make you set yourselves goals and focus your attention to specific actions and objectives.

In 1943, the American psychologist Abraham Maslow published an influential paperwork, *A Theory of Human Motivation.* In it, Maslow debated that healthy persons have a certain number of needs, and proposed arranging them in a hierarchy. He defined some needs as being primitive or basic - the physiological or safety needs - and others being more advanced; here he referred to social and ego needs.

After that, **Maslow constructed a 5-level pyramid**. The upper level hosts needs that can only come into focus once the basic needs are met. The first 4 levels, starting at the bottom, were called "deficiency needs," as a person does not feel anything if they are met, yet becomes anxious if they are not.

To discuss what concerns us the most, let's skip to the 4th and 5th levels; the ones describing the self-esteem and self-actualization needs. In order for you to get there and feel those needs, such as the craving for confidence, respect, and achievements, all the other needs placed on inferior levels should be accomplished.

Let's assume the physiological needs are being met. What happens on the security and safety, or on the love and belonging levels? Do you consider yourself fulfilled? **In this chapter, the most common life events related to the needs situated on the 3rd and 4th level will be discussed.** You will be able to read about real-life stories, as well as tips on how to settle your eventual problems caused around the Safety-Security and Love-Belonging needs.

In the following chapters, you will be able to go forward to the 4th level of Self-Esteem to learn how to set proper goals, and more to the point, to analyze the 5th level of Self Actualization; to explore the most efficient way to accomplish your goals and reach your targets with minimum effort.

Let's talk about LOVE

Jane was 29 when she met Adrian. She was already accomplished in many ways: had a booming career, a nice, modern apartment she bought for herself for which she had almost paid the mortgage, a small car of her liking and, lots of friends to keep a busy social life.

Jane knew who she was, what she liked and hated, what she should keep away from, and what goals and dreams to follow.

Adrian was a great catch. He was 31, tall and handsome, smart, independent, owned his own business, and adored Jane from head to toe in the most sincere and loyal manner. He was meant to heal Jane's memories of past failed relationships and to fill in the love chapter she could never fully decipher.

Months passed by, and Jane and Adrian were excited by each other more and more. She quit her job, gave up her new apartment for rent and moved a 5-hours' drive away to Adrian's city to be closer to him. They moved in together and were planning to live life together and make the best of it. Jane was meant to be a mother who keeps her family close, caring and sharing, building and watching over her nest. Adrian was so enthusiastic that Jane was nearer to him, he showered her with gifts and involved her in all the aspects of his life, and always-on-the-run, agitated lifestyle. He was truly happy and felt he had found his soulmate for life.

But as time passed by, Jane found herself, after only a few months of living together, that Adrian's crowded, overwhelmingly schedule, and many ideas... and even many gifts were suffocating. She craved to be loved, cared for, and to live a quiet, steady life, not a tornado of events while keeping her man's hand in the storm. Her new job was nothing compared to the career she left behind to be with him. She lost her motivation, and could not understand *why her sacrifice to be with him doesn't pay off. She began to feel miserable, and couldn't cope with his agitation. Nothing seemed to make sense of this newly built life. But, no reason to give up: she went to a numerologist... why not, maybe this kind of alternative therapy works. Then, she visited a spiritual healer, because it's nice and modern, and soothingly calming to be spiritual. When no alternative therapies actually gave her the clarity and stability she needed, she turned to more serious, traditional ways, and found the best psychologist in town to help her find peace of mind. Meanwhile, Adrian continued to live as intensely as always: he asked her to marry him; and she said yes while being haunted by the same demons of doubt and depression.*

No progress. The engagement or all the therapists couldn't bring her the clarity she craved for; the pain continued and started to reflect in the way she treated Adrian. He was no longer the prince in shining armor. He became the main reason why she felt uncomfortable and sad. She simply couldn't break his heart and leave him suddenly, yet she knew she couldn't marry him. She just avoided his presence, enjoyed more the moments she was alone and started to treat him rudely or yell at him for seemingly no reason.

The once happy love story between two beautiful, intelligent and successful young people became a burden neither of them could escape from. Both good people, but kept together not by real love, but by kindness and weakness... not to share happiness, but to create an unnecessary chain of misery.

When families are not as they should be

One late night, in February, their dad suddenly woke them up. "She is gone, she is dead, dead," he shouted.

It was a cold, rainy night continuing a series of dark, clouded and short days. The evening went on as usual. Tom was smoking and reading a book at his desk lamp in his hideaway room. His wife, Johanna, was finishing her latest painting in her creation room. The kids, Joe and Liam, were in their rooms doing God knows what teenagers are doing nowadays. The heavy rain was hitting the rooftop, and everything seemed steady and calm.

It was passed 11:30 pm when Tom decided to go downstairs and get a snack… But the loud music coming from Johanna's room was alarming. She had never listened to Joe's metal rock albums before, as she was always yelling at him to turn that awful noise-like sound down. "What on Earth," Tom whispered to himself… And, as he slowly opened her door, he saw her laying on the couch. Her heavy black hair was spread around her. She was 42 now. He had met her in college 20 years ago. He was studying engineering, and she was pursuing a major in psychology. They were both young and energetic. He could not let her go. They got married after graduation… started their careers and had worked hard to become accomplished. Joe was born 4 years into their marriage. Liam came 2 years later. They had it all - a beautiful American family living their dream life.

And, as he watched her there, laying on the old couch, he had that moment of realization. The image was vivid and clearer than any sensation he ever had experienced - she was not sleeping, not with that loud music playing in the background. She was dead, dead as she could be. The cigarette she had smoked was still stuck between her fingers... it had burned all the way to the filter and burned her index finger too. Her fingers were black and turned cold... no longer moving, she seemed serene and more beautiful than he had ever seen her before.

But when last did he actually look at her? She was meant to be there for him. Since the beginning, he was hard at work building his career at the oil company he was working for. She would return from work, prepare dinner, look after the kids, and wait for him to return each night. She was there to support him, whatever his moods might have been, whatever harsh decisions he took. She was his pillar that he hardly noticed, seldom thought about. Yes, he was faithful... but so self-absorbed, so ambitious to see his professional goals accomplished and got things "his way" that he forgot her in the background.

Now, she's gone. Why did she do it? Why didn't she say anything? Or did she? All this time? The kids are only 16 and 14 years old. They will grow up without their mother. What will he do? What will tomorrow look like?

Tomorrow is already here; it's 12:06 am. Just a few hours left until dawn. Another gloomy, dark day stands ahead of him... one like all others before, but the first one without her. Many more endless days to come...

What relationships really mean to us

Where did Jane go wrong?
What could have Tom changed in due time to foresee that his wife was at her wits end?
When do things start going terribly wrong?

Nobody can actually say exactly when relationships start falling apart. It simply happens within one's daily routine, and the moment when feelings start to go wrong is swift and slips quietly into the dark. Don't try to overthink it. Don't look back to your past in order to find the exact moment you lost control over your relationship, to analyze who said what, who was wrong or who was right. It won't give you any satisfaction when you realize that you were right while the other person was not. If you have already lost control, there is nothing you can do to change things that happened in the past.

So, look up: Is there anything you can DO to change the situation you got into? Things won't change by themselves; it takes action from your side to make things happen. Are you in a position to fight for your relationships? DO IT, before it is too late.

There's no universal recipe on what to do and what not to do. It's up to you to find your way, your path. But, be aware that there are **4 factors that can help to repair a broken relationship**:

Communication: The first one and the most important one is communication. You might disagree with your loved one on many issues. But that doesn't mean it's the end of the world, and you need to start a fight because of it. That is silly and won't lead anywhere. Find the diplomacy to approach topics that you know might be uncomfortable, and don't hide issues that could turn into frustration. Express your fears, your needs, your disappointments, your inner self. If you are loved and show kindness in the way you discuss your problems, you might be surprised by the positive feedback. Remember to adjust your tone of voice and use positive, kind and honest words. Treat your loved one the way you'd like to be treated.

Compromise: There is no other way to reach a resolution - when you disagree - if one of you doesn't eventually compromise. Yes, nobody likes to do it, but it takes two to tango on life's ups-and-downs, and you need to stick together. Don't think about compromising as a sacrifice and never, when angry, remind your loved one how many times you have done that for their sake. Consider compromising as an act of kindness and giving. Learn to give. Share happiness by being resilient and willing to solve issues, and offer others the opportunity to smile.

Sharing: When you're in a serious relationship that you care about, there's nothing healthier than sharing yourself and your life with your loved one. Love's abundance comes with time, and it's encouraged by patience and attention. When in a relationship, remember that the actions you are doing, even if alone, might also affect your partner; do not do things they don't like, even if they won't find out; and don't badmouth them with your friends or family because it was also your decision to agree about something, so you're actually criticizing yourself too. Share your time, your problems, your feelings and your goals with the one you love. You might be surprised by the ideas they can come up with in order to help you. Also, you might find amazement in the way they come close to you when you're open, talkative and honest with them.

Growing: Let's face it, you didn't fall in love with your own reflection. As proud as you might sometimes be, you couldn't ever love your reflection. Remember the first things you noticed about your loved one? It might have been the way they know how to talk to people, the way they dance, their wild imagination, or the simple and incredible way they made you feel. Find those treasured qualities. A healthy relationship is based on mutual advantages - both partners should respect and appreciate the many ways they differ, and find inspiration to improve and aspire to better themselves.

But, what happens when you have that deep gut feeling that you have tried everything and all is lost? Where does this feeling come from?

There's no way to keep a fire burning if you keep pouring water over it. To be able to succeed, to find comfort and happiness in your relationship, you and your partner need to be compatible. There is rarely such a thing as a bad person. People are born with different qualities and, upbringings and experiences, which makes us have different perspectives of how human interactions and lifestyle should be. Some might be quiet and more private, some could be loud and energetic social bees, while others find happiness in building a shelter in their family. There is no wrong and right; it's just a different approach. We only live once, and that's why everybody should be allowed the chance of finding happiness the way they choose.

Don't force your perspective of happiness on your loved one. You might hurt them, and you will also hurt yourself. If your life's purpose does not have common ground with your loved one, and you can't see eye to eye in building a lifestyle together… just give up. Shake hands in the most polite way you find possible and go forward. Follow your heart, find your inner peace and go towards what actually makes you happy. Free yourself and free the one you're unintentionally keeping captive.

Life gives us paths to take, but in the end, it's up to us individually to decide which alternative suits us better. Don't let yourself be told whom to love and how to love! Don't bend your inner values or needs for someone who can't understand you, but also don't throw away a relationship just because you forgot to communicate or pay attention to it. Face the true nature of your heart and live truthfully to yourself and those around you! Pay yourself and others the respect all people deserve!

Why the distinction between work and private life

Bills need to be paid. You can't live on thin air, no matter how minimalistic you go. In case your parents weren't millionaires, and life has already blessed you with more money than you can spend, you need to earn yourself a living.

And, as you know, earning decent pay doesn't come without sacrifice and hard work. The schooling system preaches a society based on fairness and meritocracy; through this argument: **study hard = get a good job = earn well = live well**. But is this reality?

According to a study of Jaison Abel and Richard Dietz of the Federal Reserve Bank of New York, in the year of 2010, **just 62% of college graduates had a job that required a BA**. Where is the whopping 38% of what's left working? Why did they settle for less than their level of education or why did they spend their time and money in college if it wasn't an investment to pay off?

A survey conducted in 2012-2013 by the Association of American Colleges and Universities showed that **93% of employers placed greater value on a candidate's critical thinking, communication and problem-solving skills than their undergraduate major**. The same study revealed that 95% of employers were looking for candidates who were capable of thinking 'out of the box' and had proven innovation in their activity, favoring employees who studied liberal arts versus those who were more into tech-limited activities and interests.

So no matter how much you struggled to choose a major in college, to graduate and to follow your dream of getting hired to practice what you studied, the reality of the job market might differ and make you turn to something new; a job that you might not have even considered a few years back. Because, after all, you need to earn your pay, and adapt to the society you live in. Studies have shown that it would be best to stick your new found job regardless of the maximum level of education you received. In 2016, according to the Statistics Portal, the median household income in the US according to the educational attainment of a householder could easily vary from $43,000 to $90,000 between a high school graduate and a person who has a BA.

But, no matter your level of education, a job is a job, and it should better be well done - less stress with your superior, potential promotions in the future and, a steady income for you and those who depend on you at home. Keeping a long story short, isn't this what you are usually aiming for?

And here it goes with the routine. According to the Bureau of Labor Statistics in 2015, **Americans work an average of 38.6 hours per week**. That's 7.72 hours per working day. While younger people aged between 20 and 24 spend on average 36.4 hours at work each week, people aged between 25 and 54 worked 42.8 hours each week. According to the same statistics, men work almost 5 hours more each week than a woman, up to 41.1 hours, while married men work 5.1 hours more than those who are unmarried. The differences come from social pressure; from what your group of reference or what society expects from an individual.

You'll surely feel the burden of supporting your family more as a man than a woman. Traditionally, even in the modern times, men are expected to provide. It might sound sexist, but it's common. Most women prefer men who are not childish when it comes to the couple or family's security. So, terms such as "boy toy" or "boyish charm" are pushing men to go the extra mile in their jobs. In the same manner, society considers women to be makers of a comfortable home, a place to have children and respond to the growing family's needs and demands.

But, despite all of society's clichés, families in this day and age are very different. For instance, you get to see many single-parents with very busy schedules trying to earn a living as well as being present to support both their children's material and psychological needs.

So, work is a must. Whether building your career was what you always wanted to do or not, you still need to go to work, and it's an everyday mission. So how do you manage your job, your home-family life, and your social life, while not neglecting your own personal needs?

Most of the time, work-related stress can become overwhelming, and the pressure induced by it can result in anxiety and depression. According to Bond University's Professor of Management, Cynthia Fisher's 1997 study, *"Emotions at Work: What Do People Feel, and How Should We Measure It,"* it starts easily, with the feeling of **frustration** and **irritation**. Further, the negative emotions develop into **worry** and **nervousness** and then into **anger** and **aggravation**. Then it reaches the stage where you have the feeling of **dislike** developing up to the maximum level of **disappointment** and **unhappiness**.

These evolving emotions erupt while accompanying simple events: you get more workload than you can handle; you don't like the tasks you are forced to handle; you don't get enough appreciation; your superior is yelling at you for no apparent reason; you get forced to work over time. There's no satisfaction in feeling used by a company until your energy is depleted, and then have to go home to a different set of challenges and issues that rest on your shoulders too.

That's why you need to take it easy and listen to your inner voice that will quickly signal something is wrong with you. For each of the steps described by Prof. Cynthia Fisher's study, there are solutions that are at your disposal, and that could prevent further deterioration of your general well-being.

Frustration and irritation

Frustration usually manifests as a feeling of being trapped, unable to meet your needs and wants, not being capable of going forward. You could feel frustration or irritation when you see a superior who is incompetent, when you have to wait for a project to advance, when your team is too disorganized, or when you don't get a promised promotion. When frustration and irritation are lasting for too long, they might lead to other more negative emotions. So take care, take action in due time:

- **Take a break and evaluate:** When things seem to heat up, stop and think a little. If you're feeling worn out, ask yourself what exactly is the reason for your frustration. Let's say your project has been postponed after you had worked hard to launch it. Now, try to find a positive aspect about this; for example, you will now have time to take another look at it and make sure your project is successful. Refuse to stress out about every unpleasant thing that happens to you because you can't prevent them!

- **See the bright side:** Clarify the exact reason why you're frustrated about it in your mind, and then compare it with the positive aspects of your life. For instance, if you have children and you are proud of them and their results, wouldn't it be a shame to let your temporary work situation shade the happy moments and not enjoy these to their fullest? Is it worth allowing your mind be consumed by work-related problems when you need and have love and appreciation to share at home?

- **Re-evaluate the situation:** Think about your previous experiences with frustration. How was it the last time you felt like this? Did you reach any resolution while feeling like this? Was it useful for you to maintain this emotion in order to escape the situation that triggered it? So, just stop, and calm down.

Worry/Nervousness

When situations seem to degenerate at work, and you know that the general situation is bad or your own position might be in danger, you tend to get worried and nervous. What if they will sack you? What if they add more workload to what you're already handling? Your productivity is most likely to decrease when this happens. So, take the following ideas into account:

- **Look over your surroundings:** Your colleagues are also agitated by what is happening? Do they gather in the kitchen or break room to discuss/gossip about the situation? Avoid getting into these kind of meetings that won't bring any added value. You're only going to end up increasing your nervousness.
- **Focus and react:** Are you afraid you're going to be fired? Take a break from your worries and simply mobilize your thoughts; worrying will just get you

stuck and not offer any solution. Brainstorm arguments on why your position is important for the business. Write them down and be prepared to prove to the company you're working for that you're actually bringing value to the business.

- **Keep a worry log:** If you have things that concern you for longer periods of time, start a log. Describe each of your worries and then schedule a time when you must be prepared to face them. Write down your feelings, and also write about the possible solutions, and how you're willing to apply them. You'll find greater comfort, and you'll be better prepared to face these issues.

Anger and aggravation

Don't lose your temper! Losing control of your anger is one of the most destructive emotions you could have. It might lead to unpredicted reactions that usually turn out extremely bad and can't be fixed easily. People will remember your outburst, lose their confidence in you, and you risk spoiling a reputation of reliability and respect you've build up about yourself over time. Here are some suggestions to control your anger:

- **Be aware of the early signs:** You know that moment when you start to get heated, your sight turns dark and you feel like yelling from deep inside? Well, when you feel the signs, do yourself a favor and leave the room you are in. Go somewhere else, drink a glass of water, smoke a cigarette, do whatever makes you calm down a bit; just don't burst out with rage. You'll regret it, and it will be too late.

- **Imagine yourself from the outside:** Can you imagine how you look, how you behave when you're angry? For instance, think about one of your colleagues and how they reacted when they let anger control them in public. Did you like what you saw? Did you find their approach suitable for their situation? Now try to analyze yourself and see your mimics and reactions when you're angry. Are you proud of yourself? If not... don't make a mess out of things, and restrain yourself.

Dislike

The feeling of dislike in some situation or of some person is natural. It comes after a series of experiences and it's not unusual or uncommon to want to avoid someone or something or to just give up. But, no matter how bad you feel, in a professional working place, if you show dislike as an emotion, you'll also be harming yourself, your position and your professionalism. So, here are some ideas to deal with people you dislike:

- **Show respect:** When you need to work with someone who you don't like, set aside your pride and ego. Show respect and treat the other person as you would normally treat anyone else. Just because that person might behave in an unprofessional and not-respectful-enough manner, doesn't mean you should do it too. Think about the project's success: if you're involved in it, it's important for you that it ends up well. Also, think about your image at your workplace: you want to be appreciated for your diplomacy, tact and professionalism. Don't spoil them by acting below your standards.

- **Be assertive:** When you're being treated rudely and unprofessionally, don't accept this humbly. The person who is doing this will continue to do it. Even more, others might see this and follow their example and humiliate you too. The first thing you need to do is to be assertive. Find kind, yet direct words, to address the person who is bothering you and let them know you are not happy with the way they behave, and ask them to have an appropriate conduct. Let them know you refuse to work under such circumstances.

Disappointment and unhappiness

If you reach the point where you feel disappointed or unhappy, the situation is obviously very serious and should be addressed accordingly. These emotions will not only impact your productivity and performance, but they might also expand with serious consequences over your private life, and affect the way you interact with your loved ones and the quality of your overall life. Disappointment and unhappiness trigger low energy levels, anxiety and panic, and can keep you away for any kind of professional or personal achievement. So, before you let things reach disastrous proportions, take a look at these tips:

- **Analyze your mindset:** Take a break from any disruption to take a good look at your mindset. Things won't always go your way. Accept the fact that sometimes you win, sometimes you lose. This sinuous path is actually what life's all about. You will be able to better appreciate your successes after this period of turmoil.

- **Record your thought patterns:** Write down! Always write down. What exactly makes you unhappy? Identify the exact problem by describing it in the best way you know how. When you see the big picture and all of its aspects, you will know how to act and what to do.

- **Find positivity:** It might sound a bit forced, but smile! Put yourself in situations that will bring a smile to your face. Whether you're playing with your children or watching a stupid comedy show, find something to smile about. Smiling makes the brain feel happy. It activates the anti-stress messengers and triggers a totally different state of mind. When you smile, dopamine, endorphins and serotonin are released into your bloodstream, helping your body relax, lowering your heart rate and blood pressure.

Just expose yourself to smile-generating contexts and let yourself loose.

Our initial presumption, **study hard = get a good job = earn well = live well** might not exactly be transposed in real-life situations. Studying hard increases the chances of getting a good job, but this is not a guarantee. Soft skills contribute a lot to getting a good jobs. Doing your job with passion and professionalism might set you on your way towards promotions and award you with good paychecks. But earning well doesn't mean you will also live well. Striving for professional success might be tiring and consuming. Work-related problems might easily affect your personal life and the sacrifices you make for your job might end up leaving you unhappy. Each time you experience problems at work, which are caused by your superior, your colleagues or customers, your projects; just remember to control yourself in due time.

In order for you to be able to establish clear goals and then find the strength to accomplish them, you don't need to get stressed out with your work or let it control you. So take action at the first signs of you feeling anxious or when you feel any negative emotion taking over.

The money goal

Imagine you could have enough money to travel the world back and forth, always in first class. Fancy yourself affording as many properties and luxury items as your heart desires, and at any time you want to get yourself something. What about making enough money not to have a care in the world and also being able to provide your loved ones with the lifestyle that they can only dream about? How would that make you feel?

Would you be worth more in the eyes of those who are around you? Would your neighbors, your business collaborators or your family members respect you more? Will they associate any new values to you just because they know you have a big bank account?

Money is not a goal per se. It is important to us only because people attribute a certain value to them. Money represent power - to procure things and to make us lead as an authority figure. It is valuable because people think it can bring them the things that society treasures as important. But if you think deeply about it, you can put a monetary value on most of your goals, but you can't connect such a number to an emotional level of satisfaction.

You could get the biggest house or the fanciest, most expensive car. You will feel proud and be very pleased with your acquisitions, at least for a while. In the end, you'll still sleep the same amount of hours, you'll still eat your favorite, maybe not even the most expensive brand of cereals in just "some bowl," and you won't escape your everyday problems while hiding in your luxurious mansion. Your car will drive you around to the same places you would go with any other car, and you'd still have to get out of it when you've reached your destination. You can't tie up your entire existence to money and the power that it can grant you. You can't live by breathing money because sadness, heartache, disease and other problems strike the rich as well as the less fortunate in the same way.

All our lives we've been conditioned to think that money should be an end goal. That we should chase it and slave after it, work till late hours day after day just to gain it. To smell it, to touch it lustfully with our fingertips. To waste it, share it, lose it, make it again and live lavishly through it.

Although money is so vital to pay bills and is needed to buy the things that are necessary when you are in need, it won't keep you safe or warm. People will still get old, no matter the fancy laser and cosmetic procedures money can buy. People will still get sick, and regardless of the expensive and still experimental treatments, cancer and heart attacks still cause unexpected, untimely deaths. Money can get you sex and company, but could never get you real, unconstrained, unconditional love. **Time, happiness and real feelings are still priceless.**

If you got this book hoping to help you establish and accomplish a never-ending, money-making goal, you'd

better stop reading now. Stop and quit reading because you're on a path that this book could never help you with and would never claim it could. Try something else, play the lottery, try your chances at a casino, invest in the stock exchange or do something of some other nature, not this.

If you're worried about your finances, you are searching for inner peace within you and support in others, might they be friends, family of professionals, to get you on a balanced financial plan, to make ends meet and also accumulate in order to get your life settled, you're most welcome to carry on reading. The goal here is not to rule the world and become the almighty leader of a new sect, but to become the leader, most trusted and most important, active player of your life. **Are you willing to go forward?**

Social status?

A good social status - everybody craves for it. People struggle to create for themselves a public image generally described as prestigious and honorable. For this, they compromise by attending to the duties commonly considered as right, adhere to a lifestyle praised and noticed, buy brands that are better valued over cheaper ones, and buy houses and cars with a tendency to show-off. Face it! In order to prove to others that you have a good social status, you'd need some money and some fame in your social groups of interest or community.

Some people don't have to do anything, they are just born with a silver spoon in their mouth. The money and prestige of their family is enough to offer them seemingly endless possibilities and to provide for a worry-free lifestyle. Others don't have this luck and they gain it the hard way through competition and individual effort.

What are the exact ingredients? Sadly, gender, race, and family-ties play an important role. Then, education, occupation, marital status and accomplishments are added to the equation being self-assessed. In this day and age, inherited capital tends to become less important. Governments and NGOs promote gender equality, and racism is only endemically spread and is condemned harshly. Other self-built values have become more and more important: physical appearance and dress, etiquette and social behavior.

In many cultures, social status is linked more to etiquette and morality, rather than to money and opulence. Yes, you could reach your high social status desiderate through fortune and fame, and through good relationships. And if you do so, you will need a good, well seen job and money; plenty of money in order to support your position. Yet, this is not all and it's not the only way. You can easily choose to be an informal leader in your group or community. Kindness, good will, respect and involvement pay off, and bring you more than you could think. Be kind to those around you. Offer to help - even if you help your neighbors move some furniture or become the parent who is in charge of the carpool to school. If your time allows it, offer for some voluntary work at the homeless shelter or at the retirement home. Don't harshly judge those who seem to be in a poor position and appear to be weaker than you. Life is all about ups and downs; you might end up there some day. Show people respect and take time to get to know them before putting labels on them.

How will this help you? First of all, this *"social giving"* will be rewarded with experience and life lessons. You would learn life stories of people less fortunate than yourself, and you could become wiser and more understanding. Also, you would be doing genuinely good deeds that no money could buy, the kind that earns respect and gratitude and healthy, long lasting relationships with others. So next time you sacrifice your wants and needs for money and your job, remember… besides the goods you will be able to buy in your spare time, there are other things that are much more precious and more sensible at your disposal, which could help you reach a good and healthy reputation, based on authentic values.

A story of violence

Alice had a little doll she named 'Belle'. She received it from an aunt when she turned 2. Alice slept with Belle, went to school with it, told Belle all her secrets and befriended it, while Belle helped Alice the best way a rag doll could - had been faithful for 6 years and kept up the best it could, needing sewing only twice - and Belle was needed.

Dora and Dean met in high school; they were high school sweethearts. They were young, foolish, and in love. Dean was a bit of a bad-boy, and Dora loved that about him. Her mother tried to warn her about him... but she was way too fiery to listen to her. Dean graduated and took a job at the local garage, while Dora had to drop out before finals as she got pregnant. They never married, even after Alice was born, but they rented a trailer and tried to make ends meet.

As years passed, Dean realized his small wage wouldn't cover all their needs. There were bills to be paid, food to buy, his woman always asking for more, and a child who needed so much. He simply knew it... he couldn't handle it. He couldn't do it, he couldn't escape them... the overflowing bills, his woman's constant nagging, the small child's crying, the miserable place they called home. So he started drowning his sorrows in a couple of beers at a local bar each night after work. It was just an escape from reality. But escaping reality and fogging your mind is too tempting when there's seemingly no alternative, so the couple of beers started to become half a dozen per evening.

Dora didn't see this coming. When she was 17, she imagined life would be a rock-and-roll style fairy tale on a motorbike. She had no idea what responsibility or parenthood meant. And she didn't foresee that her knight in shining armor would become nothing but a drunk; coming home late and angry, threatening, cursing and hitting - cause his hand was heavy when intoxicated. And as the misery in their life grew, so did Dean's anger.

Misery was everywhere - on their plates, in the cheap clothing, in their thin and rusty walls and their shaky furniture, in their eyes of hungry greed of the many things they wanted but knew they couldn't afford. Oh, Dora how she complained… to her mom, to her best friend, other women in the neighborhood, or to her sister late at night on the phone. She just kept on complaining… and with each word he overheard, his blood pressure would rise and his sight became darker. Rage, pure rage was boiling within him, waiting to erupt.

Meanwhile, Alice watched them from behind her blue eyes, wishing she could become smaller to fit better into her hiding place that she had started to outgrow. She had her little safe spot right between two kitchen cabinets. She sat there, while daddy was yelling and hitting mommy, while mommy was crying and yelling back at daddy, with her eyes closed, with her head on her knees and with Belle by her side.

After each fight and after the alcohol began to fade from his system, Dean would promise Dora "they would make it somehow". And Dora never questioned nor gave this promise a second thought. There was no other reality beyond what they had built for themselves; it was the only one they ever knew.

What to do when there's no way out?

Did you ever feel like Dean: **trapped, angry, lost, feeling like taking it out on others for the overwhelming misery?**

It's normal to feel this way sometimes, when life has been too hard on you. Yet, the normal choice for most people is not to be violent. Violence comes out as an extreme behavior, and leaves deep, hard to heal marks on both the assailant and the victim. It is your kindness and goodness that - when at your lowest or deeply hurt by someone - you choose not to be violent; you pass through your sorrow with dignity. Find those positive qualities in you and work on them to become that what defines you best.

There is no such thing as the end of the line. As long as you are alive and healthy, somewhere inside of you - without you even knowing it - exists the necessary strength to carry on, to improve yourself and your life. Giving up is just an excuse you can't afford to make, especially if you have a family depending on you. Letting yourself fall prey to negative feelings will only eat you from the inside out. The everyday worries, responsibilities, and limited possibilities might be overwhelming; nevertheless, use your sense of reason. Breathe. Don't let yourself be floored by negativity.

Think about the consequences of giving up! If you've reached the conclusion there's nothing else you could do, your disappointment, and think that the lack of opportunities is permanent, in what does it reflect? Will you be able to support your family and loved ones with the proper care? No, you won't! The stress will affect your power to focus, your patience and even your clear judgement. Will you be able to set an example to your children? Will your situation improve by itself? No need to calculate anything here - the answer is simple: with no change in the situation, nothing will improve.

What do you do? You start over. It's easier said than done, but it's possible. That's why you began reading this book and that's why you're on the way to gaining clarity of mind; gathering strength to move on, and doing what's best and fair for you. You'll soon discover what are the most important things in life to set goals towards, and how to maximize your chances to achieve them. So, reset. Eliminate the negativity and let's go.

Different ways of experiencing death

It was a warm day in May that they had scheduled for the funeral service. The light was joyous, and the cemetery had that pale, vivacious shade of green only spring can offer; the one that starts to fade away into a deeper, tired shade once the summer heat waves strike.

Only 9 months ago, everything seemed perfect. The entire family met up in Florida for a short vacation, to enjoy the ocean and each other's presence. There was laughter and fun... the kids were playing in the sand, the adults enjoyed their jokes and late evenings together. Everybody was happy.

Jacob was 57 and had a full life, with ups and downs, successes and big failures; just like everybody else. Firstly, he married while being quite young. Acted like a fool, but gave his best to be a provider. Things just didn't work out, so they divorced amicably 5 years later. He tried to fix his life and married once more, this time to a much younger girl. Sue was cute and her young blood made her energetic and hardworking. They lived happily for a few years. They welcomed Jack, their first-born. Then, 5 years later, Linda was born. Both children were beautiful and smart, coloring their parents' life with joy and fulfilment. Times were also good. The factory paid Jacob a good wage to support a family of 4. Sue was a good loving stay-at-home mom, and on most evenings and weekends their house was always full with family and friends dropping by for a good home-cooked meal or a chat. Their dining room saw lovely soirees, lots of people having fun and intense debates and life stories being told over a glass of wine until the late hours of the night. There was no lost soul or friend in trouble that Jacob wouldn't have opened his door to, or offered shelter and comfort. Sue was not necessarily a smart woman, but worked with the energy of a man, and rarely questioned anything related to their lifestyle. She was happy that the children were healthy and doing well in school, their money was enough to put food on the table and a reliable man like Jacob was taking care of the family. She would nag him for many things, although they were all without great importance, and lacked the capacity of any deeper thinking or intense emotional vibe. Yet, things were in motion and looked good from the outside. Noah was their 3rd and last child, 14 years younger than their first born Jack... a surprise pregnancy. They loved Noah all the same, a little miracle that no one was expecting. Their life seemed to have everything they might need and the everyday normality was enough for them.

And everything, until 9 months ago, seemed to be just right. They all met up in Daytona Beach. Jack, now 29, brought his wife and their 2 daughters. Linda came with her husband and their son. Jacob and Sue brought 15-year-old Noah. Nobody was surprised to see Jacob catching a cold. It was not unusual. But the cold didn't go away for weeks after returning home. Two months after the first symptoms, Jacob finally gave in to his wife's usual nagging, and went to see a doctor. And after doctor no. 1, he needed to see doctor no. 2 and then doctor no. 3.

That late November, doctor no. 3 called both Jacob and Sue into his office for a certain and definitive verdict - metastatic lung cancer. No doubts, no treatment options, just alleviatory measures. Jacob was quiet and didn't complain. He spent the next 6 months between his home bed and the one in the hospital. Sue took the news with surprise in the beginning, and with sadness and denial... but accepted it fast enough in her simple way as "meant to be" and "it's God's will", while continuing to act normal. People came to see him, not staying long... not to bother or tire him, or simply because it's awkward to be at ease near a person waiting to die.

At his funeral in May, most of the people Jacob had been kind to came to pay their respects. He went as he lived, surrounded by people, warmth and light.

Sue coped with the grief in the best way she could. In less than a year, she had found another Jacob - in a much older widower - to her oldest son's outrage. She needed to continue her work around the house; to feel useful and not to break the chain. So a man to feel safe with and for whom to show her emotionless attention manifested through good meals and a clean house was all she *needed. Linda gave birth to her second son 3 months after the funeral. She refused to get involved in the mostly speechless, cold conflict between her older brother and her mom. She hid her grief in taking care of her two very young boys.*

Jack refused to accept a man's existence could be wiped away by death. In his mind, Jacob was still there, still as present as always through the lifestyle that he preached: the kindness, and love of life and people. He continued to visit his mother, for his teenage brother's sake, and then shout cruel words at her to Noah's nightmare. Noah took time to adjust to the new situation. Although their house seemed untroubled and another man eventually took over, moving in and fulfilling the duty of man of the house with a subtle presence that granted Sue the looping normality she craved for, Noah dropped out of high school. His wound was meant to heal in much later years, in his late 20s, when he made a family of his own.

It took a couple of years for Jake to accept his mother's rushed decision to move on without a tear. Sue lived longer than her second husband, old enough to raise both Linda's and Noah's children, to suffer 2 strokes and one heart attack. Until the day she died, she went to both her husbands' graves to pull out weeds and bring flowers for each religious holiday she held dearly.

When stories end and new ones begin

Some are more fortunate and don't have to experience death until late in their life, when nature takes its course and the older generation - grandparents, parents - pass. Others are forced to experience grief earlier, prematurely losing their parents, siblings or loved ones.

Death doesn't end the emotional connection or the relationship one had with the person who died. It's normal to continue to have feelings and to feel hurt. Death only changes the relationship from one that might be physically dependent to one that is strictly emotional and spiritual. It's normal to experience emotional numbness, sadness, anger, abandonment, regret, anxiety, depression. Every person has their own way of mourning and recovering after such a shocking and profound experience. Some mourners openly express themselves to others, sharing the pain and their stories. Others, more stoic, try to escape the tension by getting involved into activities that will help them think about something else - whether they are doing house-related chores, exercising, working on a hobby, studying a new courses, or voluntary activities.

People who have experienced the death of a loved one are not their usual selves, and there's nothing wrong with not feeling good or one's usual self. If you've lost someone dear, you might have problems to concentrate or in focusing on anything else but your loss, and you might have a slight impairment in your thinking and remembering abilities. The stress caused by grief could also affect you in a physical manner. Mourners are more likely to have physical problems, get sick and be in accidents due to a weakened immune system and a lack of focus. It's best that if you are in mourning to avoid activities that require a high attention, such as driving or high precision tasks.

According to psychologists, **grief can be experienced even after many years**. These episodes are usually triggered by special occasions such as tastes, songs, scents or stimuli that might remind you of the person you lost. Although present, the episodes of grief lose frequency and intensity as time passes.

If you have gone through the loss of someone dear to you recently; here are some suggestions that might help you ease the pain:

- **Join a support group:** Many people find their peace among others who have been through a similar experience. They feel it's easier to communicate here in expressing their worries, their fears and their real feelings. Hospitals, churches or social service agencies are usually in charge of organizing such groups. Try go to a meeting. You're not forced to talk about yourself if you're not comfortable with it. Just attend and see how it goes.
- **Go to counseling:** A professional therapist is able to offer you a personalized, individual help that could help alleviate your pain and help you cope with your grief. You might not want to speak between four walls with a new person and reveal the way you feel. Still the comfort a therapist could bring is worth a try.

- **Acknowledge the feeling/learn to cope with the change:** It's very normal to go through sadness, sorrow, anger or guilt. Don't be afraid to recognize them and sometimes even express them. It takes time to heal and you need to be truthful to yourself in order to do that.
- **Be patient with others:** When you are in pain, you might say inappropriate things to those who are closest to you or those who might even try to help you. Don't lose your temper and don't be offensive. People who are next to you in times of sorrow are the ones who you should keep near as they are the ones who truly love you and want to help you.

If one of your closest friends or family members is experiencing grief, it's time you take responsibility and show your support. Be calm, be patient, listen without being judgmental, and give support where you can. It takes time, but time heals.

Chapter recap

In this chapter, you have been introduced to Maslow's Pyramid of Needs. This American psychologist defined human needs in a hierarchical structure; these are:

1st level - Physiological needs: breathing, food, water, sleep, shelter, clothing.
2nd level - Safety and security needs: health, employment, property, social abilities.

3rd level - Love and belonging needs: family, friendship, intimacy, sense of connection.

4th level - Self-esteem needs: confidence, respect, the need for unicity, achievement.

5th level - Self-actualization needs: creativity, morality, acceptance, need of purpose, experience, and accomplishment of inner potential.

This book's purpose is to get you on track to establish the most relevant goals you have, and then to offer you the best solutions and tips to see them accomplished. You can easily set yourself the goals your mind and heart desire, if you are able to reach the fourth level of the pyramid, the one related to self-esteem. In addition, after setting such goals, later in this book you will learn how to achieve those goals through organization, and accomplish your goals in a manner that won't require too much effort.

In order to progress to the goal setting and goal achievement stages - meaning the fourth and fifth level of the pyramid - you need to make peace with yourself. In this second chapter of the book, you've had the opportunity to explore how people are usually put down by the most common, yet impactful issues of life. These may be related to love and family, broken relationships, the continuous yearning for money and social status, the huge hole left by acts of violence, or by the death of a loved one.

You need to remember that life isn't and never will be perfect. You will have to experience the death of a loved one, as all people do. Not all your love relationships will be perfect, no matter how hard you try. Your family might not be the way you want it to be. Your current job is not exactly what you dreamed of when you were in school. You might wish you had more money than you are making. You need to understand that this is part of life. It's normal to feel tired, anxious, or unmotivated sometimes. It's also fine to experience that feeling of anger erupting at times.

All you need to do is to embrace life for what it is. Darkness has its own meaning - you can't see the stars in its absence, can you? Breathe, don't let yourself be conquered by negativity; try to eliminate the people or habits that do you harm if you know your entire existence doesn't depend on them. Breathe. Be yourself.

Killing the monster

Killing the monster

Defining the enemy

There is a pain, an ache harboring inside you. Sometimes, it is so dark, it's pulling you down. This monster of sorrow gathers all the negative experiences you have faced in your life. It vividly remembers the countless times your parents told you "No" as a child. It is the disappointment and the unworthiness you felt when your 4th grade teacher said you were not good enough to participate in the fair for which you prepared for weeks. The same monster hides the sadness and anxiety you felt when you had to give up on your first relationship and it grew with your memories of unrequited love.

It is turning and twisting inside you, feeling your every move. You see its red cunning eyes watching you. It feeds on your indecisiveness, it triumphs over your mood swings. It plays with your uncertainties, each moment you feel trapped and confused, when you don't know what to do and you're trying to search for an easy way out. It is there, getting stronger, making a statement each time you simply can't find the energy to be productive. You are consumed by the fear of failing and each time you are allowing for your self-image to be neglected.

You could say it shadows your heart with frustration and anger. It is there because of all the repetitiveness, boring things that happen each day, that bore you and seem to lead to nowhere. It's also there because of all the responsibilities you have to carry on your shoulders. All the people, family members, sometimes friends, coworkers, your superiors at work, who just need something from you. They want a part of you, one that would fix their issues, solve their problems and needs. Yet, it found the ground to hide and develop inside you due to all the ups and downs of your life, the scars left by all your moments of unhappiness, your failed challenges and broken encounters.

In the end, it is you who created it. And now, it is the one that leads you and controls your life. It is the one responsible for your sadness, for your reluctance to challenge or change, for your anxiety and depression. The monster and you have become inseparable. It feels like a drug and feeds on its host every time bad impulses occur. How are you going to handle it? Can you tame it? Can you release it to the wilderness and forget about it? Are you two even separable?

It starts with a change

If you want to set up big goals in your life, the monster that is living inside you must disappear. The sooner it happens, the better. It will try to come back, it will try to pull you back from your path and will use its tricks of fear, lack of motivation and frustration.

If you know deep inside you that you need a change, you will understand that you need to modify what is currently affecting you and you realized that the life you are living now is not what you really want…

Or, if you feel that something is missing and you won't be complete unless you follow your dreams and do something else, and that means changing significant aspects of your lifestyle…

…Well, you have got to face that monster, reject it and speak out.

You will not be pushed to change yourself but guided to adapt to change. People who change out of the blue, going from left to right in just minutes, usually fail their own values. No, you won't be forced to change your beliefs or core values. Those are what distinguishes you as a person and make you special and unique. You will be required to change your mindset and to perform certain activities that will somehow force you to adapt to performance, stability, and a positive way of thinking.

You will be encouraged to love yourself. There is no other way. Look in the mirror and think about what you see. Some wrinkles where you don't want them to be, maybe? Did your hair start to turn gray? You never liked the shape of your nose or your mouth or you don't like what you see? That's a trap the monster wants you to fall into! Don't be tricked. You are a unique creation on this Earth. Even if you have flaws and you're not perfect the way you want to be, it doesn't matter as there is no one out there like you. Did your physical aspect ever make people not love you? Look at yourself and think about last time somebody confessed their love to you. Was it this morning? Did your life partner said he or she loved you? Did your children said they love you before going to school in the morning or last night when you tucked them in? Or, if nobody declared their love to you recently, you surely had a relationship at some point in your life. Someone saw you as beautiful and appealing because you were unique to them. So, if others can see it, why can't you? Love yourself for who you are!

You will be shown how to think as a winner. You'll discover how to use the Law of Attraction in a specific way. The Law of Attraction states that, whether you realize it or not, you are responsible for bringing into your lives both positive and negative experiences. In order to use this concept in your favor, you need to understand that where you place your focus can impact your life and what happens to you. For instance, if you spend days in regrets and whining about something you lost and can't regain, the negativity you draw on you will reflect also on other aspects of your life. What the Law of Attraction actually does is to simplify for common understanding some psychological concepts. While reading and trying to go forward with this book, you won't be required to use the Law of Attraction in an irrelevant manner. If you want a red Lamborghini, just doing nothing and thinking intensely about it, won't bring you your dream car. You will be guided to adjust the situations you get yourself into and the energy you use, in order to keep you focused, ambitious and efficient.

What is the thinking pattern of a winner?

How do winners think and feel? Confident people are the ones with some kind of allure that distinguishes them from the crowd. That attitude they are displaying is not in any way tied to arrogance, but success in what they do, confidence in whom they are, and the choices that they make.

Winners don't avoid clear answers, they know when to say NO.

You're a grown up. You know what works with you and what doesn't. If someone is asking for something from you and you're not completely comfortable in saying yes, don't lie to yourself. Don't push yourself into doing or accepting something you don't like and don't mumble and answer. It's either "Yes" or "No". If you avoid an answer, you may show uncertainty, lack of power and you will unwillingly invite the other person to enforce their point of view. So, if you don't agree with something, just say "No", in a smart way.

Here is how:

- **Be assertive and direct:** Don't apologize for something that you don't like to do. Don't start with *"I'm sorry, I can't..."* If you are not sorry, don't say it out of courtesy. You can be polite without making it

seem like it's your fault you're not agreeing to
something.

- Set limits: If you feel the need to explain your
  decision, make people understand how much you
  can or are willing to help them when you refuse their
  full request. If, for instance, someone is asking you to
  help them with their project at work and tend to
  overwhelm you with tasks, tell them exactly what
  you can help with and how much you are willing to
  help.

- Be firm: If your negative answer has not been clearly
  understood and the person is trying to make you
  change your mind, don't return to your decision. Of
  course, your first answer should have been well
  thought and you didn't say, "No" just for the sake of
  saying, "No". So, if you know you took the right
  decision of refusing someone, remain firm.

Winners don't question their actions, they take decisions.

Sometimes it may be hard to choose from a multitude of
alternatives. Yet, life forces you to do it in order to go
forward. Do you get that, *"What if"* feeling sometimes? What
if you chose something else? How would it be? What if the
option you made won't work? What if you had not hurried?
What if you said what you had to say in a different way?
The truth is there are so many IFs in our lives. We would go
crazy to think about all the possibilities we say no to and all
of the opportunities we might have missed out.

So, how do we avoid being regretful about our decisions?

- **Evaluate the pros and cons:** When you are in the situation of choosing between two or more alternatives, make a list. Do it in the comfort of your home. Do it on a piece of paper or in an Excel spreadsheet, whichever you prefer. If you have to take a quick decision, draw a line in your head and start adding pros on the left side and cons on the right side for each alternative. Think about immediate gains and also think about long term consequences and implications.
- **Have a life philosophy:** Does the decision you are about to make respect your life's values? Are you pleased with what you chose? Will you continue to be at ease with your decision in a week? Would you choose the same thing in a month? Does your decision respect your inner values that lead to your very existence?
- **Don't look back:** You've done what you thought was best, you took the best decisions you could. Now, you just have to stick to it. Make it work. Don't look back, don't think about the *"what if"* scenarios. You're responsible for your decisions and you need to show intelligence, tact and determination in what you do. There is always something to learn from, no matter which path you chose to go on.

Winners don't close doors, they open new ones.

Look at big success stories. Let's take the Harley Davidson case. William Harley and the Davidson brothers pieced their first motorcycle in 1903, in a backyard garage. They only produced 3 units of their innovative motorcycle in 1903 and only 8, in 1904. Steve Jobs and Steve Wozniak started the Apple business in a garage too. Referring to it, Wozniak said: *"The garage didn't serve much purpose, except it was something for us to feel was our home. We had no money. You have to work out of your home when you have no money."* Walt Disney began his success stories also in a garage. He used it as an animation studio for months after arriving in Los Angeles, in 1923. The truth is, nothing good comes out of thin air and in order to accomplish something, find the best ideas, the best way to make them possible, you need to start from somewhere.

Here's some great advice on how to keep yourself open to possibilities:

- **Don't judge harshly:** The first impression always matters. But how many times did you fail with your first impression? Don't harshly judge anyone or any idea before you learn more about them. The story or details behind may make you radically change your mind. Also, how would you feel if you yourself are tagged on the spot with no right of appeal?
- **Don't stop believing in your ideas:** People may say your idea is useless, that it has no solid ground. But do you feel like you're on the edge of discovering or inventing something? Don't stop. Until you can't

prove to yourself you are wrong, go on, follow your dream and don't stop believing in your power to change the world.

- **Embrace failure:** There is rarely such a concept as failure. When something you wanted to do didn't work out, take time to analyze the feedback to draw a conclusion. You may have invested a lot of resources and things didn't turn out the way you wanted. Analyze why. Think what you should have done differently and how you would do it if you have the chance to take it again from the beginning. Learn from your experiences.

- **Keep experimenting:** Hardly anyone gets it right on the first try. In most scenarios when your goals are ambitious, you need to practice. As the saying goes, *"Practice makes perfect."* So, no matter how many times you failed, carry on, learn from your failures, make the best of your mistakes, adapt through the knowledge you've gained and move on.

Winners don't stay put and quiet, they act and they create.

Nothing falls down from the sky, as a God sent present. You should play the lottery if you are waiting for this to happen. In case the odds are not in your favor, you may need to wait for an entire life for that *"something"* your heart longs for. Are you willing to leave your dreams and needs to fate or are you going to step in and make things happen?

Here is how you can favor odds on your side, without great effort:

- **Give up on Netflix:** A confident, action driven person won't spend their life hiding in some time-consuming, no result activity. Nothing against Netflix, reading fantasy novels or playing computer games, as they are all good entertaining activities that help you unwind at times. But if they become a time-consuming habit, you have a problem. You are wasting the precious time of your life chasing images and stories that are not real. Once you close the computer, the TV or the book, you'll wake up to the same reality you most likely want changed. It's time to act and consider time as a precious resource.

- **Make an agenda:** Be organized. If you know what you want, act accordingly. Make a list of what you need to do, of the things you need and split everything into manageable chunks. Set realistic deadlines and do your best to reach them. Sometimes you may find yourself in an unpleasant situation because you skipped a deadline. Don't punish yourself. Continue until you get things done. Each time you successfully complete a milestone, don't forget to reward yourself. It will do you good and encourage you to go forward.

- **Put yourself in the middle of things:** As already discussed, good energy attracts good energy. It's the same thing with mindsets. If, for instance, you know your goal is to become the best contemporary jewelry designer, study the art of jewelry design. Take an online course. Go a step further and attend classes dedicated to this. Make friends among people who share the same interest. Use your spare time to study other arts, such as painting or dance, improving your artistic and emotional sides and later transpose them into your work. Think about yourself as whole, you are what you do and everything that you create is a reflection of what you envision your life to be.

Winners don't cheat the system, they are truthful to others and themselves.

It is highly likely you will never become a pro in mathematics if you had problems with it since you were in middle school. Not everything is meant to be conquered by everyone. The world itself is beautiful due to its diversity and the fact that people are different and each unique in their own way. You can't change your true nature and reach peak performance in a field that you're not gifted in. Also, you can't buy or cheat your way up. Eventually, people will find out. The mess that you have created may have far-reaching consequences and then you will have no option but to retreat and sadly, some people never recover from it.

When you're aiming for something big, remember:

- **Do it with passion:** You've got higher chances of reaching your goal if it corresponds to your inner potential. What's that talent that lies inside you? Maybe you're a person with a keen eye for design and proportion. Maybe you're musical. Maybe you're a good planner and your organizing skills could make things happen. Probably you are a good listener and can help in the world by offering good advice and guidance. Every one of us is gifted and better at something than others. What is your top skill? Explore it, embrace it, and apply it when you set up your goal.

- **Always improve yourself:** No matter how good you are at something, accept that you're not the best in the world. Even if you were to be recognized as an authority in your field of competence, there is always room to be better, to learn more, to reach another level of knowledge and competence. You have the duty to constantly learn and show your experience through what you want to accomplish.

- **Respect others:** An achievement is fully recognized as long as it has been accomplished in a fair and respectful manner. Make sure that the path to your hopes and dreams is the correct one, doesn't negatively affect anyone, and it respects the moral criteria society imposes.

- **The sky's the limit:** If you are confident and focused, there is nothing stopping you. Live each day to its fullest, dive into opportunities and prove yourself. Be good, balanced and wise and push for new limits, as the sky's the only one. Challenge yourself and go on your path to success with an open heart.

Do you feel like a winner? Do you have that motivation that would kill the bad energy monster that lies inside you? Are you willing to take your life into your own hands and act right now, fairly and loyally to your dreams to your true self? Read further to find out how to set your goals in a clear manner, but also to discover stories of people who created success when all hope seemed lost. **Be inspired and stay confident. You can do it!**

The power of transformation

Nora is now 41 and a single mother to her son, Nathaniel.

She has always played by the book. She married young, while still in college, out of blind love. Things looked promising in the beginning. They were both young, in love and full of dreams, like most newlyweds. Both she and her husband, Damien, were pursuing a career in law, struggling to stay in school, while also paying the bills and coping with the newly found responsibilities of married life. Eventually, Nora dropped out, took 2 other jobs and worked days, nights, weekends, to get the money their family unit needed in order for Damien to finish school, take his exams and start working himself.

For 6 long years, Nora worked as an office assistant by day, as a freelance copywriter by night, and as a shop clerk during the weekends. Her jobs were all different, yet they were all necessary in the financial struggle that overwhelmed the young family. Meanwhile, Damien remained loyal to his goals. He finished law school, started to practice and, ultimately, he opened his own office. Fate was finally smiling on them: a good income, a large house, a new baby, good social status and an overall nicely settled, beautiful and successful all-American family. Dora could finally breathe; no more extra hours, supplementary jobs. All she needed to do was to be an assistant at Damien's office. The job allowed her to look after Nathaniel, go to painting classes as a hobby, and still look smashing at social events they were invited to.

The story could have ended here. But, as often happens, years passed and the monotony settled in. Days began to resemble each other more, and this was not enough for the ambitious Damien. He felt like he deserved more than life had to offer and that he was destined to get whatever his heart desired. First, he bought 2 sports cars. Then he changed his wardrobe and joined a select private club. In the end, he had a young lover, a beautiful, tall blonde. She somehow looked like his wife, only 15 years younger.

Nora quietly accepted all the changes her husband brought to their life. She knew that his opulence somehow came from the frustrations they shared when they were young. She also knew that they both changed and barely resembled the young, hopelessly romantic, and full of dreams couple that shared every thought. But what she didn't expected was to return home earlier one evening to find a beautiful 20-year-old woman in sexy lace lingerie in the middle of their kitchen pouring cocktails, when nobody else but her husband was home.

Hell broke loose. Nora wanted an immediate separation, with full custody and half of their properties. What she didn't realize was

that she would not only face her husband in the court hearings,
but also a rigid system of law and Damien's other lawyer and
judge friends. In the end, she was penniless. She did get
Nathaniel's custody. However, there was no money, no roof over
their head, no job.

Her parents were long passed away. Her sister was not around
either; she had moved to Australia, years back, with her
Australian, somehow weird husband, taking aunt Janine with
them. So Nora had no family to rely on. The friends she made
started to leave her too. Many of them were just the wives of
Damien's co-workers. Others were just social butterflies who
didn't want to be associated with "Poor Nora" after her downfall.

There she was. All alone, with a 9-year-old son to look after. With
her new accountancy desk assistant job at a local grocery store, she
could barely afford rent, some food for Nathaniel, and the school
supplies. The evenings were long and painful. There was no way
out. Absolutely no way out. Whom could she turn to? Who would
help? What job could a college dropout, with working experience
in a field no one would hire her in this little town, could ever get?
What future could she provide to Nathaniel in terms of stability?
How could she show him confidence in everyday life and how
could she compete with the way Damien was spoiling him? She
simply felt doomed for being naive and believing, entrusting her
life to one man. Doodling on a piece of paper on the kitchen table
one day, Nora came up with an idea. She followed her idea, in
order to earn some money to pay the bills. Her natural talent in
drawing and years of courses paid off. She began to work as an
independent illustrator. Her first contract was a mandala coloring

book for adults. The second, was a children's book. Editors were hiring her and in a 6-month period, she began to earn more as an illustrator than with her regular job 9 to 5 job.

"There may be some hope, somewhere," she said to herself stepping out of her apartment, on the way to the grocery store one clear, cool spring morning. For the first time in months, she felt that the air was more breathable, the daylight become enjoyable and the sun warmed her up. As she was walking, she stopped in front of a tattoo parlor. A sign on the window read, "Help needed. We are hiring". She knew nothing about tattoos and therefore never had the curiosity to find out. With her confident spirit, she returned to the tattoo parlor the next day to show them her portfolio she had built over the years and to tell them more about her successful illustrating job. Impressed by her fresh ideas and creativity, the owner hired her.

Nora is 41 now. She has been divorced for 6 years. Last May, she opened her own small tattoo parlor on the other side of town. Customers return to her and bring new people in as her creativity is unique and her style ranges from wild to elegant in a subtle manner. She still has no tattoos of her own, but she surrounded herself with competent people who help her drawings live on her clients for years. Her success paid for a large house she rents out now, a nice car, good food, courses, camps and vacations for Nathaniel, who's now in the 10th grade. Overall, Nora is doing well. She worked for 2 years in the tattoo parlor where she accidentally found a job opening. She learned the business, she spent late hours perfecting her technique, and moved on. She made *it. She has been seeing someone for the last 6 months and she thinks she may be in love. Yes, there is hope.*

How to establish your goal

You may not be at the stage of life where it is that easy to learn or you are time poor and need the essentials. So, you will be presented with a step-by-step approach on how you can establish your goals.

First of all, you need to fully understand **what a goal is and why you need to sketch it in a proper manner**.

A goal is a measurable ambition set up for being achieved within a deadline, that requires effort. The measurable aspect is what distinguishes a goal from a dream, hope or a need. In order to establish and follow a goal, you will need to take into consideration 3 aspects: **motivation, exact goal, achievement**.

Motivation is what keeps the fire burning. It's the catalyst that you need in order to start setting your goal. It will act like that inner force that drew you to read this book, to the curiosity of wanting to modify something in your life. Motivation is the powerful desire to do things. It can also be tricky and temporary. Sometimes, so you need to be aware that, in order to actually establish some goals, you may need to keep yourself motivated for a longer period of time. How would you do that? You need to find a good reason that resonates with your values and your objectives. That reason can be material or symbolic, but it should be able to respond to a need of yours that doesn't disappear overnight.

The exact goal is that exact element you hope to accomplish and would fix the need or desire that gives you the motivation to carry on. As described earlier, the goal is quantifiable, can be attained and requires more effort than a usual day by day objective.

Goals can be classified as:

- **Academic goals:** When they relate to obtaining a qualification or certain knowledge in some field of study.
- **Career goals:** When you want to reach a certain level of expertise or wish to be promoted in a new position.
- **Financial goals:** When you wish to earn a certain amount of money at a given point in life.
- **Creative goals:** When you want to acquire a certain level of competency in a creative or artistic activity.
- **Family related goals:** When you have exact expectations about how your domestic life should be like in the future.
- **Physical goals:** When you want to successfully practice a certain sport or a physical activity.
- **Ethical goals:** When you wish to get involved in a public cause that won't necessarily bring you any direct gain, such as volunteering for a cause, supporting local events or political issues.

The achievement is not necessarily the peak of the mountain, but the long way to reaching it. Think about it as a journey that will involve some effort, but which you'd like to be as short and pleasant as possible, without diminishing the end results. This issue, being important, will be covered in the next chapter of this book. Now, let's return to the step-by-step goal setting method.

Step 1: Define what you need

A. Write down your need

There is something out there that made you end up in the situation you're in right now. Something is bothering you. That monster inside you has been twisting and turning and doesn't let you sleep well at night. So, what do you need to do to feel better? What solution or accomplishment would change your life for the better making you happier? Is it a new job or a new job title? Do you need to master a skill? Write this down in no more than 6 words. It should look like: *"Master piano skill"*, *"Become a project manager"*, *"Lose 10 pounds"*.

B. Describe the desired result

Now that you know what you want to accomplish, you need to find that strength that will keep you focused on your goal, the motivation. Write down, under your desired end result, how accomplishing it would make you feel. Use all the attributes you need and don't worry if it's scribbled and not a well-written script or some kind of poetry. The reason you are doing this, is because you need to see for yourself if the goal is enough to keep you motivated in the long run.

C. Look over the resources

If you know where you're heading towards, you need to make a list with what you need for your effort to be a successful one. Prepare to gather your resources. Let's say, for instance, that you want to master how to play the harmonica. You could add on your list items such as owning a harmonica, downloading some online courses, enrolling in a harmonica course, making friends with some people with whom you can practice playing in private, making time to practice each day, buying music sheets etc. Don't worry if your list is messy, doesn't seem too organized or has no logical structure. You just need to write as many things as you can think of that could help you reach your goal.

Step 2: Analyze your plan

A. Determine your secret weapon

Dive deeper into your soul now. What is that quality or talent of yours that could make things work smoothly and would differentiate you from others who, let's say, have the same goal in mind? If your goal is to learn a musical instrument, do you have a good ear for music? If you plan to get a certain job, do you have the complete set of skills that would get you there? If you have them or you're working on them, why don't you also focus on the soft skills that may help you with a potential job interview or being diplomatic and making relationships in your line of work? Think about the extra mile you could go based on your qualities that could make the difference. Don't think that you're not special and you don't have anything extraordinary in you.

Everybody has certain qualities, but most people forget about them in the hassle of everyday life. It's now time to prepare and get hold of all the resources you've ignored before. Write down the manner in which you can go that extra mile in your goal.

B. Set a deadline

Your motivation may bring you far, but it won't last forever. You have a goal, not a dream. You will act, not daydream. So, set a reasonable deadline for your goal to be achieved. You may be thinking of months, or a few years, but you need to have a deadline to force yourself to act in a timely manner. Write down your deadline.

Step 3: The SMART model

The SMART model will help you challenge your goal. It's a good way to analyze if what you want is meaningful and if it can be achieved. To go through it, you will need a new piece of paper to write on and also the list you've made while going through steps 1 and 2. Take your previous notes and check if your goal is:

- **S: Specific**

In this stage, you will need to develop sub-goals based on your goal. Let's say, for instance, you want to raise a certain amount of money by next March. In order to do so, you will need to cut back on some of your spending. Spend less on fast food, pay less on clothes etc.

- **M: Measurable**

How do you know you're on the right track, if you're not measuring it? Continuing the example with saving up money, you need to do a little math. Let's say you want to put aside $6,000 in one year for a one-week trip to Paris, France. Good! Now, look over at your bank statements or receipts from at least the last 3 months to check your spending habits. How much do you usually spend on food? How much do you spend on entertainment or on cosmetics? Let's say you spend $400 a month on entertainment which includes magazines, going out bowling, watching sports games, movies, meeting up with friends etc. If you cut back your budget to half, in just one year you'll save $200X12, meaning $2,400, only by seeing less movies at the cinema, going out just once a week and giving up on magazine subscriptions. Create milestones every 3 months, to keep you on track. Remember, that this is life, it can be unpredictable and you may need to readjust the values. Alternatively, things could go smoothly and you could reach your goal sooner than expected.

- **A: Attainable**

Don't set a goal that is impossible to reach. Most likely, you won't be the first settler on Mars. Also, you may not win an Oscar in 2 years' time. Besides being realistic to yourself, you need to also make sure that your goal narrows down to a specific thing. *"Be a guru of music"* is too broad a term. Narrow it down by mastering a specific music skill, such as vocals or the guitar.

- **R: Relevant**

Make your goal relevant. Make sure that both your goal and your sub-goals on which you're building milestones are relevant to your life. This means that if you're doing your best to follow them, your efforts will make a difference in your life. Pay particular attention to the sub-goals you're setting. They all need to lead to the final goal, not to be there just to make your life harder.

- **T: Timed**

As already discussed, goals and sub-goals need to be defined by deadlines. Make sure your deadlines are realistic and you can stick to them. Sometimes you may get distracted or certain events may interfere with your schedule, without you being able to foresee them in the beginning. Keep away from temptation and go on, don't lose course.

Step 4: Review

You are nearly done. If you reach this step your goal plan should look similar to the example below. All you need to do now is to go one more time over what you wrote down and make sure you keep it as a commitment.

Here is an example of what the first three steps look like if you have followed them properly:

Recap: Step 1: Define what you need + Step 2: Analyze your plan

Goal: Be an accountant in a Fortune 500 company
Goal description: I have always been good with numbers. I've already worked as an accountant assistant and I feel good about it. I know the pay will be higher if I'm an accountant and that's why

I'll obtain my Diploma in Accounting and Finance in a couple of months. I want to join a Fortune 500 company and prove I'm sharp, I'm good at what I'm doing and I can also be accurate. I need to prove myself and find recognition for my work. It will be the first time I'd get a job in a big company and I want to learn about the corporate culture. I don't mind wearing a suit and a tie, I actually feel good about it. I want to show I'm neat and have an office job. I'm tired doing accountancy for coffee shops and having a boss who's always moody and likes to micromanage me. I want my fiancée to be proud of me and to prove I can support a family.
List of resources: *Diploma of Accountancy, top notch resume, persuasive cover letter, letters of recommendation, accounts of different job vacancy websites, at least 1 hour each day to look for job openings and submit my resume.*
Secret weapon: *Soft skills within the interview. I know I'm not the only one looking for such a job. But compared to others, I've always been reliable and dependable at work. I'm going to have the soft skills necessary to show this at my interviews and to persuade potential employers.*
Deadline to accomplish the goal: *1 year from now.*

Recap: **Step 3: The SMART model**

Specific: *YES - Get a job as an accountant in a big company. I need 1 month to get someone to help me build a smart resume and cover letter. I need 1 week to update my LinkedIn profile. I need 2 months to complete the Diploma of Accountancy. I need 3 months to apply for at least 40 jobs. I need to invest in my soft skills for at least 2 months. I need 2 interviews after which I need to analyze* *the strategy I used. If I'm still not hired, I need another 2 months to apply for at least 40 more jobs in neighboring states.*

Measurable: YES - I have a threshold for some of my actions. I also have a clear list to check.

Attainable: YES - I am qualified to occupy the position that I'm aiming for.

Relevant: YES - I plan to get married next year. I need money to support a family and build myself a career. Also, getting this job would make me feel accomplished.

Timed: YES.

Writing professional resume + cover letter: By the 30th of May.

Updating LinkedIn profile: By the 7th of May.

Graduate from school: By the 30th of June.

Improve soft skills with online courses and practicing them with friends: By the end of July.

Apply for at least 40 jobs: By the end of August.

Go to at least 2 interviews: By the end of October.

Apply for at least 40 jobs in other states: By the end of November.

... list open, based on results.

If you have everything written down, now do yourself a favor and ask yourself a few questions meant to shatter any doubts you may later have about your goal.

1st Question: On a scale of 1 to 10, how strong do you believe you can keep the motivation flame burning until you reach your goal?

2nd Question: What is the first thing you'll do after you accomplish your goal?

3rd Question: In case you fail, are you willing to try again? If yes, how are you going to start?

4th Question: Will this goal come with any eventual regrets if attained?

5th Question: If you don't start chasing this goal, do you think it will still be on your mind 6 months from now?

Chapter recap

Setting up a goal is not a difficult mission. You now have the tools that you need in hand. Before you use them, it's extremely important that you understand that any setback you may have is normal. You are a normal person, with ups and downs, with responsibilities and problems and feelings that only you know about.

On the other hand, you are unique in your own way. It's only in your power to use the motivation flame that burns inside you, and kill that monster of sorrow which tries to pull you down. You will be able to do it if you can adapt to change, while believing in yourself, your strength to change the world, and follow your dreams. The entire secret of your success stands, besides using an organized method based on measurable results, in your attitude to think like a winner. You need to understand that being firm, keeping yourself open for opportunities, not losing time, always creating and playing by the rules is the way to go. It will eventually lead you to success, as this is the only way.

Using your motivation as a catalyst will make you embark on a journey towards the exact goal and that will put you on track towards achievement. The way to achieve what you want will be discussed in the very next chapter. In this chapter, you've been given a short plan on how to makes sure you set up a correct, measurable, trackable goal that responds to your needs and you could follow on a longer term.

Remember the steps:

Step 1: Define what you need
    A. Write down your need
    B. Describe the desired result
    C. Look over the resources

Step 2: Analyze your plan
    A. Determine your secret weapon
    B. Set a deadline

Step 3: The SMART model
    A. Specific
    B. Measurable
    C. Attainable
    D. Relevant
    E. Timed

Step 4: Review
Continue to read in order to see how your goal can be accomplished in a proper timely manner, without wasting resources or energy.

Go for it!

The attitude that makes things work

Being organized is something some people are born with, while others simply don't feel comfortable organizing their things. It is who each one is and it's part of their personality and education. Now, you need to pull yourself together and focus sharply more than ever. You've decided you want to accomplish something, to go somewhere, so being organized will shorten the way and maximize the results. Still, how do you enforce the *"organization skill"* within you?

See it clearly!

You will need inspiration and you'll need to keep that inspiration going on for a long period of time. You need to remain focused and on track. Sometimes, the vision you have in your mind related to your goal may fade away in the face of common responsibilities and tasks of daily life. That is why you need to visualize your goal, your objective, in the way that you can see the actual benefits or the fulfilling feeling you'll get when you reach it.

In order to see what you're aiming for each day, add a picture that inspires you in your room. For instance, if you are aiming to play an instrument, don't only go to classes and practice it at home. Add a poster of a musician who is playing that same instrument and who you admire in your room or a place where it is visible more than 3 times a day. If you're planning to lose weight or accumulate a certain amount of money, write down that amount and post it in a highly visible place. You can also add pictures of people who have the number of pounds you want to reach or, if money is your goal, add picture of things that you could buy with the amount of money you want to raise. Make sure you visualize the importance of your goal and how much it means to you. It will help you boost the motivation and pull yourself together when your energy levels are low.

Tell people!

Presenting your intentions to those around you, family and friends, could have a double positive effect on you. On one hand, most of them will try to encourage you, to support you, and even help you. Take advantage of this and use the help you're being offered, without letting others do the hard work for you. It will be mentally easier for you if those who matter most to you approve your plan and support your cause.

On the other hand, telling is like a commitment. If you started to tell people that you are pursuing a path, following a goal, you will be more likely to actually do it and not give up. The simple reason is that you don't want to create the impression that you talk about things you can't actually do. You'd feel ashamed to enthusiastically talk about your plans and how everything should work out your way, only to quit later and have to tell the same people you were wrong. This means that telling others what you want to do is a social commitment. In a way, talking to people will constrain you to get the job done.

Get inspired!

What motivated you to choose your goal the way you did? What are the values that stand behind it? You need to get connected to them and expose yourself to all sorts of activities and people related to them.
Let's assume that your goal is to become successful in a new position at your job. Along the way, in your plan, you may need to work harder, develop new skills, go the extra mile or pay more attention to social interaction. Surely you will have clear, measurable actions to take in order to achieve all these, but it would help you more if you have examples to follow.

There are many successful professionals out there who may inspire you with their values and perspective over life. You live in a digital era, where information is just a few clicks away. How did Steve Jobs make his empire? What guided Richard Branson to build the Virgin Group? How did Mark Zuckerberg manage to build his powerful network at a young age? Follow their path as an example. You will see that they struggled. At times, they had downfalls in order to raise and to succeed; but their success generated the wisdom only experience can give. This wisdom allowed them to come to certain conclusions about work ethics, social interactions and human values. So, read their biographies, their books, follow them on Facebook, Twitter and understand the winner's philosophy.

Draw it as you mean it

This is the part where you need to get down to business. Take a wall calendar and write for each day what you need to do within the sub-goal you are working for and the amount of time you want and afford to dedicate to that specific action. If there are multiple actions spread across multiple days, just use different color markers to write them down. This will make it easier for you glimpse what you need to do over the week and month. It is advisable not to get too specific about an action at a specific hour. Instead, only write how much time you want to spend on performing it as some days may be hectic and you may have other commitments. Your kids may need your help for a school project or they may need a drive somewhere, your boss may need you for some extra hours or you may fall ill. Don't let the inherent, unpredicted everyday events distract you from your goal.

You may think that the above simple actions are not much and wouldn't have a high impact on your everyday life? You may look back and see that the calendar is what brings you structure and organization, while the other pieces of advice only work for your motivation. So, why is there apparently so little effort on organizing yourself and so much emphasis on the mind set? The reason is **solutions are not necessarily universal**.

There are certain theories and practices that apply to everyone, while most theories will be unsuitable for most people, without being customized. You can't fully copy a set of values or someone else's full behavior or schedule and expect to reach the same results, under similar circumstances. You have different skills; your reaction is different to other people under certain conditions and you have your own personal limits. **Building yourself the correct attitude, being drawn to your purpose each day and committed to it, will help you create specific favorable habits.** With good habits, you will be able to unlock an enormous power within you that can help you go further than you think.

The power of habits

Did you know that Apple's current CEO, Tim Cook, wakes up at 3:45 am? Pepsico CEO, Indra Nooyi, gets up each day at 4 am, same as the former first lady Michelle Obama. Jack Dorsey, co-founder and the CEO of Twitter and Square, wakes up at 5 am. Why would these educated, successful people put pressure on their lives and start their days so early?

The psychological reasons standing behind this apparently harsh schedule is easy to understand:

- **There are less distractions when most people are still asleep.** You will be able to focus better and also observe how the world awakes and begins a new daily cycle.

- **You will have a sense of control.** During the early hours of the morning, you won't be bombarded with calls, meetings, emails, demands. It's just you and what you choose to do.
- **You have a better willpower.** A rested, morning brain will function better than one which already started the day and is tied up in activities, choices, and decisions.
- **You can set a tone for the entire day.** It's easier to make a short list of things you want to accomplish during the day and the attitude towards them when you are alone and undisturbed.

Let's assume you're not an early bird and you can't follow this otherwise psychologically recommended habit. What should you do in your life in order to make the goal reachable, enjoyable and, most important, an easy process?

First of all, start basic: Sleep and eat.

Sleep like a baby. A normal adult should sleep for at least 7 hours a night. If you sleep less than that, in the long run, you could face mental issues such as depression. Over 90% of patients suffering from depression also complained about their sleep quality. Incidents at work or in traffic are also often related to the lack of sleep. Poor quality or insufficient sleep leads to poor performance and low drive, making it difficult to cope with daily tasks and responsibilities during the day, as productivity, cognition, performance and power to focus are significantly affected. On the other hand, good sleep can improve problem-solving skills and enhance the memory performance. Even if you're not one to get up early, make sure you go to bed at an appropriate hour. Sleep for at least 7 hours and wake up rested, efficient, and able to focus on your mission.

According to science, people who suffer from sleep deprivation have a bigger appetite, which leads them to eat more calories than necessary. Sleep deprivation is a factor of disruption for the daily fluctuations in the appetite hormones and can cause a poor appetite regulation, including higher levels of ghrelin, the hormone that stimulates the appetite or lower levels of leptin, the hormone that suppresses the appetite.

Which leads to the second problem, your diet. According to a study published by in *Cell Metabolism*, two groups of mice were put on the same diet. One group had access to food all day long, the other one was fed with the same caloric intake, but only during the most active 8 hours of the day. The study revealed that the mice of the second group were 40% leaner and had lower cholesterol and blood sugar levels. That means that eating when you're most active could be a better idea, than eating food late in the evening when you get home.

When talking about dinner, nutritionists recommend not to eat for at least 4 hours before going to bed. This allows enough time to start the digestion process and have sound sleep. To boost your focus and be more efficient in what you do, you should enjoy regular meals. Eat food rich in iron and zinc. Both are known to improve memory and concentration (oysters, fish, chicken, nuts, whole grains, brown rice, red meat are examples of these foods). Increase the intake of vitamin B (vegetables, legumes, yeast spread, wheat germ). Get more omega-3 fats (tuna, salmon, prawns, calamari) and drink at least 8 glasses of water each day.

In the end, you're not being told to dramatically change your life or to go on a diet. Just sleep well to be able to use your full brain power the next day and pay attention to what you eat to make sure your nervous system functions properly so that you can be at your best.

Second, connect to your needs: Meditate and get inspired.

Bill Ford, chairman of Ford Motor Company, Oprah Winfrey, chairwoman and CEO of Harpo Productions Inc., Arianna Huffington, president and editor-in-chief of Huffington Post Media Group, Ray Dalio, billionaire and philanthropist, have something in common: They all meditate.

"In meditation, I can let go of everything. I'm not Hugh Jackman. I'm not a dad. I'm not a husband. I'm just dipping into that powerful source that creates everything. I take a little bath in it. Nothing has ever opened my eyes like Transcendental Meditation has. It makes me calm and happy, and, well, it gives me some peace

and quiet in what's a pretty chaotic life" says actor Hugh
Jackman.

Meditation can help in significantly reducing stress and
helps with post-traumatic stress disorders. It will also make
you sleep better, feel less pain and fight against anxiety and
depression symptoms. Many people consider meditation
increases their energy levels, improves focus and enhances
the creativity and thinking abilities. According to ancient
beliefs, people are multidimensional beings, more than just
physical bodies. Spirituality still teaches that in order to be
truly happy and live a fulfilling life, people should be able to
access the subtle dimensions beyond their physical body. If
physical balance requires healthy eating, exercising, good
sleep, mental and emotional balance result from the
intangible being; they are a positive and conscious form of
decision making. Meditation can balance the way you
interpret for yourself the values and the world you live in,
making you feel calm, peaceful, deep and focused.

Don't worry if you're not a typical spiritual, religious or
very calm person. If you haven't experimented with
meditation so far, you can give it a try. You won't know if
it's helpful for you or not, until you actually try it for a while
and then you can draw your own conclusions. All you have
to do is to give yourself 10 minutes per day for this activity.
When you are alone, in a quiet, comfortable environment,
adopt a relaxed posture and pay attention. Focus on your
breath, the air that fills your lungs, exiting through your
nose, the sensation it produces. Don't think about your

worries or daily concerns! Just breathe and be aware of your body, of the way your hands and legs feel while you are sitting relaxed on a chair or cushion.

If it's too difficult for you to start meditating, use a little help. There are numerous apps you can download on Google Play or App Store, that will act as daily guides for your meditation sessions. Search for: Inscape, Headspace or Timeless.

If, in the end, meditation doesn't seem to be a solution for you, there are, of course, other ways to get inspired. Expose yourself to people who share your values. Get in touch with communities of people who aim for the same goal, who face issues similar to yours. Read success stories of people who have been through what you're going through and learn from their experience. Use your mind and your soul as a sponge of positive energy and let yourself be carried away in the direction you are too aiming for. Don't spend your time with people who drain your positivity and stay away from activities that just waste your time. You need to integrate into a flow of good vibrations, of people who embrace the same goal as you, who share your values, and live within and through this good energy.

Finally, focus on solutions: Find out what works best for you and do it.

You need to understand that you are not a robot that functions by the clock each day, week after week, month after month. You won't be able to sleep for precisely 7 or 8 hours each night. You won't be able to eat your veggies each day at 1 pm sharp, neither meditate for 60 days in a row. What is important is to stick to your good habits for more than 90% of the time. If you're well-rested, going to bed at 3 am one evening and getting up 4 hours later won't be a shock or a disaster to your system. The system has enough in-built resources to attenuate the impact of lack of sleep for one night.

Don't expect to form new habits out of the blue. It was thought a new habit forms in 21 days, according to an idea that became popular in the 1960s. Yet, researchers from the University College London, consider that it takes an average of 66 days to create a habit. They reached this number in 2009, when 96 participants in a study were asked to say how many days they needed for a new activity to become a habit, meaning automatic. The participants were asked to perform various routines, such as waking up at a specific hour, doing exercises, eating certain foods. Don't get discouraged. 66 days is just an average. Of course, you can form habits faster, and in some cases in 2, 3 or 4 weeks.

In the end, there is no universal solution. It is scientifically proven that some habits, such as the ones mentioned before, sleeping, healthy eating, meditation and exposing yourself to a mind flow and values similar to yours are more likely to have obvious positive effects. But, the way you adapt them to your needs and your way of being, as well as how you introduce in your life various changes that help you be more positive, focused, and more efficient is still up to you.

You have to know yourself and be aware of your limits, your likes and dislikes, your mental strength and capacity, as well as your body's own pace and necessities. It all starts with respect for what you are and who you are. Accept yourself and half the battle is won.

Chapter recap

There is no hocus pocus magical formula in the way you should be organized in order to make sure you accomplish your goal. If you expected a magic formula or doing something extreme to solve all your problems overnight, you are not being realistic and thinking about a shortcut. This is not the attitude of a winner.

In order to reach your goal, you need to be realistic. You need to visualize it, as it is, and constrain yourself to it through a healthy, organized routine. A good sleeping schedule and healthy meals are important, as your mind will need to be well rested and your body to be healthy, so that you can focus on what is important to you.

Putting yourself in the spotlight and drawing strength from the positive vibes from your role models, your family and friends, groups of people who share your same interests will help you simply breathe in the values that are important for you and therefore commit to actions that will help you be ready in your goal reaching project.

You are not a mechanic, by-the-clock being. Embrace the fact that you are human and benefit from emotions. You felt it deep in your bones you need to go on a path that, in the end, will make you happier, wiser, better. Then, you had the courage to ask for help and even read a book on this topic. You feel the need to improve yourself and grow as a spirit, aiming for higher purposes. It's true you need to build yourself a calendar you will closely follow, so that, step by step, get to complete your sub-goals and achieve your final, higher purpose. But, understand yourself! Personalize your daily routine in a disciplined manner where you are focused on your needs, with your pace of doing things and on the way you know it works best for you.

Have faith and act. It can be done.

QA:
risks and safety nets

QA: Risks and safety nets

For all the times you may feel lonely

There will be times when this goal chasing experience may make you feel lonely and discouraged as others don't share your enthusiasm and your energy. There will be times when you will feel like quitting as you feel your work and the pressure you're putting on yourself are all in vain. You will think and feel no one sees, appreciates or supports you.

You may also wonder what happens if you fail?

- What if, no matter how hard you tried and how well-set you felt your goal was, the final result is not the one you hoped and worked for?
- What do you do then?
- Who is to blame and what path should you turn to?
- What if things degenerate on the road and the elements on which you've build your plan are no longer up to date?
- How much time are you allowing yourself to spend on your goal?
- How much is considered to be an investment and how much does it take to become a loss of time or an obsession?

Don't be discouraged! It's normal to go through a multitude of feelings and it's also normal to feel lost and a restless soul.

The dark monster of anxiety may want you back and is pressing its sharp claws on you. You have the winner and can-do attitude seeded deep inside you without even realizing it. As a human being, you have been gifted with free will and the power to create. You have the ability to distinguish right from wrong, to analyze and to take decisions. Based on what you consider most inspiring, more than any other living being, you can act and create wonders starting out of thin air, being motivated only by the ideas you have generated.

Don't be afraid to try, to get involved and to fight for your beliefs! In the end, you have nothing to lose!

Frequently asked questions

The following is a series of questions and answers meant to help you focus, ease your mind and be prepared for unexpected situations you may encounter. Please go through them as they will help make the entire goal achievement process smoother and less daunting.

Q1: How do I know my goal is a good goal?
A1: There is no such thing as a good or bad goal. No one can tell you what is best for you other than yourself. You know better what you miss, what you want and what you aim for. As long as achieving your goal brings you satisfaction, comfort, and improves your overall well-being, the goal is a good goal. If you want to know if a goal is correctly set, define it one step at a time, as you have read in the goal

setting chapter. This reduces the chances of you failing in your mission and will also help you be prepared for the next step.

Q2: How long should I work for my goal?
A2: Usually, if it takes more than a year it's a no-go. That doesn't mean you shouldn't have long-term plans for longer than a year. But, if you want to be precise and establish actionable sub-goals, set yourself clear milestones, aim for reasonable goals that take less than a year to complete. The surrounding circumstances under which you organize your plan today may change due to various factors. The economy may go through a downturn, you may need to change your job, your daily schedule may also need to be modified, and new responsibilities may appear. These circumstances have the potential of changing your daily life and affecting your plan towards the goal. Still, you may ask yourself what happens if your one and most important goal, realistically speaking, requires more than a year. The best thing to do in this situation is to break it into reasonable rewarding milestones and enjoy each one as an individual goal. This gives you the benefit of feeling satisfied because your efforts have paid off, while also adapting each milestone to changing environmental conditions.

Q3: What happens if I miss a deadline?
A3: It's not recommended that you end up in this situation. When you establish your plan, be realistic with the timeframe you'd need to accomplish each sub-goal. If you think you could have trouble sticking to your deadlines add

a comfort margin of maximum 15% when you make your plans. That means that if you know your sub-goal would require 2 months, meaning 61 days, add an extra 10 days for comfort. Don't use this 15% margin as a trick for all your sub-goals, as you may get too comfortable or even lazy. Still, if you miss a deadline, it's not the end of the world and you should not give up on your dreams or your goal. Simply reschedule everything or try to catch up on the next sub-goal. You may face unpredicted situations/issues. What is most important is not to give up when trouble comes your way.

Q4: What do I do if, as time passes by, my goal loses meaning?

A4: According to the Bureau of Labor, people have an average of 12 jobs in their life. That means that for 12 times people need to change the group of people they're spending 8-9 hours per day for about 5 days a week. They need to adjust to a new company`s values and requirements and to adapt their day-to-day schedule to the working schedule. To change 12 times takes quite an effort and this is only related to a career and the job-related environment. If you add up the family adjustments or the friends that come and go in your life, you'll realize that only for reasons that concern others, not your own individual needs and wants, you have to change for dozens of times. When it comes to what you want, building yourself up as an individual, finding what suits you best, you will also modify your habits and lifestyle a number of times. That's why, a well-chosen goal is not one that loses meaning over time.

There are 2 situations you need to be aware of. On one hand, if a goal truly loses meaning, it's an extreme situation and it was not compliant with your needs and your true self. That is why you've previously been asked not to set goals that take more than a year to accomplish. The reason is you don't want to waste time in case your life turns 180 degrees. On the other hand, if, in time, you start to feel like nothing makes sense, hold your breath and don't quit that easily. You embarked on a mission, it's only natural to face challenges and get tired sometimes. The negativity monster dies hard and will try to pull you down. Don't let it do it, you're stronger than it and you know it!

Q5: Are there any situations when I am allowed to give up?
A5: Usually, no. You are an adult, a responsible person, who has thought it well through before choosing a goal and going forward. If you feel like quitting, it's because good things in life come for a price: hard work, ambition, determination and persistence. Don't lose focus, don't lose track. Your efforts will pay off. Yet, there are special situations when you should quit and don't feel sorry about it.

This could happen if:

- Your goal becomes a real discomfort for other people.

- Your goal transformed into something that was not meant to be. It went completely off track and there is no way you could go back and fix it, as it already proved to be dysfunctional: Your sub-goals had consecutive unhappy results that made you make mistakes in your private life, costing you happy relationships or your job.
- A radical change intervened in your life: You moved to work to a new country or something extreme happened that changed your values and landmarks in life.

Q6: What is the next logical decision/action if I fail?
A6: There is no such thing as failing. If you didn't reach the expected results with your plan, there must be a good reason to justify this. You will need to find out what it is. You will truly fail only if you don't search for closure and you don't learn anything out of what you've been through. If you want to hide the mess under the carpet, it means you're willing to take the easy way out and all you did so far, all your efforts, was actually in vain. If your goal was not accomplished, go back on your path and see where things went wrong. Was it a planning issue? Was it a wrong strategy? Did you follow what you wanted to do or not? Did something or someone severely interfere with your plan?

After you discover what went wrong, write down with as many attributes as you can the reason your plan failed. Also, on the same paper write down what you would change if you could go back. Thinking only about the problem that made you miss your goal won't help you too much. Finding a solution is what would revolutionize your thinking and would make you successful next time. If your goal is still haunting your soul, you should try again. This time, you'll surely succeed.

Q7: Will I be considered a loser/failure if I give up or I fail?

A7: The answer to this question depends on whom you're expecting to answer. Those who love you and support you would never consider you a failure. Those who don't understand you and your motivation may consider you lost a battle, as they didn't support your efforts in the first place. What should you personally think about yourself? As discussed in the previous question, you should consider this has been a lesson. You are now wiser and better prepared. It's true that you lost time and put some effort that didn't help you as you expected. Yet, in life not all things turn out to be exactly the way you have envisioned it to be. This doesn't mean you need to give up or put yourself down. You are not a loser, you are not a failure! You're ambitious, hardworking and becoming stronger and smarter with each experience that you gain!

Q8: How should I explain my goal and what I need to do to achieve it for my loved ones?

A8: It's important to gain support from those around you. It will help you feel more confident, motivated, and comfortable with what you have set in mind. In some situations, it may also prove to be useful, as they may offer a helping hand. After you know exactly what you want to achieve and have your plan written down, try to explain to those who you hold dear why spending time and investing resources in achieving this goal is so important to you.

If you are married or in a relationship, you will update your partner with your needs and your schedule, as you would like them to approve and support your future actions. When you approach your loved ones to explain your intentions, make sure you pick the right moment. If you suspect they'll struggle to understand and accept your decision, pay even more attention to the moment you pick for what you have to say. Prepare to reveal your goal and further plan in a moment when both you and the person you want to talk to are both calm, open to each other and not pressured by noise or any immediate responsibility that wouldn't allow you the time to discuss on the topic. Focus more on what this goal means to you rather than focusing on what you think they would like to hear. In that way, you will use the power of empathy. People who genuinely love you or care for you will want you to be happy and will usually be there for you.

Q9: How should I cope with the lack of support from my family or friends?
A9: Again, as already stated, things don't always work out the way we intend them to. Sometimes, family relationships of friendships may not be as easy as you would want them to be. No matter how hard you try, some people won't understand why a certain goal is so important to you and

why you are willing to sacrifice your time and invest in something that for them, doesn't even make sense. If your goal is an ethical one, doesn't hurt anyone and respects the common rules, you have every right to go for it! Yes, it will be tougher for you without the support of your loved ones. But some people are stubborn and only see things their way, no matter how much they care about you or how nice they are. You should not quit just because you don't have the full support of your family or friends. Try to listen to them and see why they don't believe in your goals. Take it as feedback. If you think you should go on your way, go ahead. The inner motivation is enough to keep you going. You have the power to do it even alone.

Q10: Is there a right or a wrong way of doing things?
A10: Yes, there is a right way to do things. The right way is already provided by the method, in the goal setting stage. You just need to seriously go through every step of the process. There are many wrong ways of doing things. An incorrect way is one that would put your needs above other's needs or would harm people around you for you to gain something. It's not fair to gain happiness and satisfactions on other's suffering or pain. Remember the Law of Attraction, what goes around, comes around. Another wrong way would be to search for quick fixes. Usually, everything that you fix by sticking band-aids will eventually loosen up creating a mess even after you have built upon the *"temporary bandage."* So, it's best to take more time and think things through in order to have a solid foundation.

Q11: Does the method described in this book offer any guarantee?

A11: The answer to this question is a big and simple NO. Are you waiting for someone or something to take over the responsibility of your actions? If you plan to become better and to improve your life, you need to be aware of who you are as a person: What are your strengths and your weaknesses? What can you do and what you can't you do? There is no one, no matter how close or supportive, who could fix your life, fight your battles and provide you with the enjoyment and satisfaction you could get from doing things by yourself for yourself. All this book did was to provide you with a simple, clean explanation of how the human mind works and a method that should significantly reduce the risk of failure when you set up your mind to something. With this book, you have received a structure and some examples that should be useful for you to follow and be inspired by. The fuel that makes the method work are actually your drive, strength, confidence, and motivation. If you have those, sooner or later the results will show!

Q12: Is there a safety net for what I'm doing?

A12: Do you need a safety net? You will provide yourself with the safety net. If something doesn't go the way you planned it, you should know how much time, money or other resources you are willing to invest and possibly lose. Of course, there is a pace of doing things. Some people are faster, some are slower. We all work at a different pace. You can also work on the speed of your project, to create comfort. But is this what you're actually aiming for, a safety net? Are you willing to restrain yourself from revealing your true talents, energy, and determination, to make sure you are as safe as possible? How much of the power and authenticity of the plan would simply be wiped off by the fact you don't want to step out of your comfort zone? No, you should not go on the extreme to risk your health, your home, to jeopardize a functional relationship or put at stake your life's savings. Yet, don't get yourself tied up by unnecessary constraints. You need to feel confident and free in order to access all the power filling your soul and to act wisely so that it can help you get where you want to. You don't need a safety net.

Final word

Final word

The farewell moment

It's now time to say goodbye. During the course of this book, you've been given a few stories. What you didn't know about them until now is that they are all true and come from real life events and experiences, even if a few elements or names have been changed. In case you felt you have something in common with any of the characters, it goes to show that your problems, no matter how twisted, are not singular and there is a good chance for you to solve them. Also, clear instructions have been laid out so that you can set up a goal in an authentic and trustful manner and follow it until it becomes your reality.

Besides the templates and the psychological explanations, what you should remember most of all after you read this book is that: **The power to improve yourself and your life is actually in you**. You don't need any new, fancy, experimental method. You don't need sophisticated and expensive counseling or oriental practices. All you have ever needed lies within you and you've been carrying that resource with you for as long as you've been here. It's all about faith. It doesn't matter if you're a Christian, Hindu, Muslim, Buddhist or belonging to any other religion. But, just as some pray to a superior force governing the laws of the universe, distinguishing and balancing the right and wrong on this earth, based on pure, spiritual faith, now it's the time to have faith in yourself.

Your upbringing, whether happy or not, all your experiences which turned out to be successes of failures left their mark on you and transformed you into a unique human being. You have the power to either make people laugh or have the option of being cruel and create pain for those around you. You may have experienced both alternatives at some stage in your life. This power to bring joy or to create sadness is often ignored or underestimated. Just think about it! When was the last time, even though it was a small gesture, you've helped someone? Just think about that moment and relive it in your mind.

So, if you can do that, why not turn to yourself now and start things right? If you can influence others, love them, create pleasant moments for them, it all starts with you. You owe this much to yourself. First, becoming wiser and stronger for yourself is the key ingredient, in order to share your enthusiasm, your joy of life and wisdom to the world. Think about yourself like a glass full of water. If the glass overflows it means it's full, you'll have the resources and the energy to give back. If it's almost empty, you won't have enough even for yourself.

Start believing in yourself. Start acting and create a world of good vibrations with you at its core!

Resources:

https://www.lovepanky.com/love-couch/better-love/how-to-fix-a-relationship

https://www.statista.com/statistics/233301/median-household-income-in-the-united-states-by-education/

https://www.washingtonpost.com/news/wonk/wp/2013/05/20/only-27-percent-of-college-grads-have-a-job-related-to-their-major/?utm_term=.9a90d9b80ab0

https://www.mindtools.com/pages/article/newCDV_41.htm

https://www.forbes.com/sites/ashleystahl/2015/08/12/six-reasons-why-your-college-major-doesnt-matter/#1dacca1935a0

https://www.thebalance.com/what-is-the-average-hours-per-week-worked-in-the-us-2060631

https://www.neuronation.com/science/benefits-of-smiling

https://www.britannica.com/topic/social-status

http://sheerbalance.com/10-ways-to-remove-negativity-from-your-life/

https://cdv.org/2014/02/10-startling-domestic-violence-statistics-for-children/

https://griefminister.com/2014/03/12/the-5-major-ways-grief-changes-the-whole-person/

http://victimsofcrime.org/help-for-crime-victims/get-help-bulletins-for-crime-victims/grief-coping-with-the-death-of-a-loved-one

http://powerfulmind.co/things-confident-people-dont-do/

http://www.thelawofattraction.com/

https://liveboldandbloom.com/10/career/how-to-make-a-big-decision-without-regret

https://www.skillsyouneed.com/ps/setting-personal-goals.html

https://www.forbes.com/sites/glassheel/2013/03/14/6-ways-to-achieve-any-goal/#5a2667266406

https://www.thebalance.com/how-often-do-people-change-jobs-2060467

https://medium.com/personal-growth/this-is-when-successful-people-wake-up-835a6a289f29
https://www.healthline.com/nutrition/10-reasons-why-good-sleep-is-important#section2
https://foodwatch.com.au/blog/energy-boosters/item/eating-for-exams-what-to-eat-to-boost-concentration-and-memory.html
https://tmhome.com/experiences/famous-people-who-meditate/
https://www.huffingtonpost.com/master_charles-cannon/why-meditation-will-chang_b_5930440.html
https://alifeofproductivity.com/meditation-guide/
https://www.digitaltrends.com/mobile/best-meditation-apps/

Thank you again for reading this book.

We trust it helped you gain confidence and provided you with the tools and inspiration you needed.
If you enjoyed the lecture, we invite you to search for more books from the Moon Rise Temple collection or to visit our design portfolio on Behance at:
https://www.behance.net/Cobrasan

Made in the USA
San Bernardino, CA
30 June 2020